BART STARR: A BIOGRAPHY

BART STARR:
A BIOGRAPHY

Gene Schoor

Doubleday & Company, Inc., Garden City, New York

ISBN 0-385-11694-2 Trade
0-385-11695-0 Prebound
Library of Congress Catalog Card Number 76–56332

BART STARR: A BIOGRAPHY

It was 16 degrees below zero the morning of the National Football League championship game between the Dallas Cowboys and the Packers in Green Bay, Wisconsin, December 31, 1967. For the second time in two years the Cowboys and the Packers were to meet to determine the championship of the NFL and the right to play the American League champions in the Super Bowl.

It had warmed up to 13 degrees below zero by game time. The fourteen miles of underground cables and wiring that were meant to heat the field, were almost completely useless, and the turf was hardly anything more than a sheet of ice. Under such conditions, with traction almost impossible, it was going to be difficult to run the ball, to block, to tackle; the furious gusts of wind that swept the field would make it almost impossible for the opposing quarterbacks to mount any kind of accurate passing attack. It was going to be difficult for the ends and backs to run their proper pass patterns, to cut, spin, and maneuver for those important forward passes. To add to the difficulties for both the Cowboys and the Packers, there was a fourteen-knot wind blowing down from Alaska, resulting in a wind-chill factor of 40 degrees below zero. Holding on to a sizzling, spinning forward pass, in that kind of cold and wind would be next to impossible.

The players, on both squads, studied the weather conditions and the frozen turf and knew what they were up against. So did the 50,861 fans who came out in that bitter weather to cheer their team on to victory. Green Bay fans are utterly amazing. Bundled up in furs and blankets and stocking hats, except for the few who had to leave every now and then to warm up their cars before the gas lines froze solid, they shivered in the stands until the last whistle ended the game. The millions who watched the struggle on television throughout the nation were, to say the least, a great deal more comfortable in their living rooms and neighborhood bars. Wherever they were, at home or at the game, the fans were about to witness one of the greatest games in the history of football, and the most brilliant game that Bart Starr had ever played.

The Packers were dressed in their regular silk football pants and extra-long wool stockings. They wore their thermal underwear as well as extra sweaters over their underwear shirts. Most wore thin, woolen gloves.

"I could use an extra pair of those gloves," said Jerry Kramer, the Packer lineman.

"We'll need extra pairs," said Chuck Mercein, hard-charging fullback, who had come to Green Bay from the New York Giants.

The Cowboys, who were less accustomed to the frigid temperatures than their Wisconsin rivals, were freezing.

They had to keep on the move constantly to keep warm; they rubbed their hands and kept searching for some warm spot that might shield them, give them some protection, however slightly. They were chilled to the bone. Some of the players muttered, "This is crazy! How can you play football in this kind of weather?"

But they played, and they played very well, though it took them a while to get their game plan moving.

At first, it was all Green Bay.

The Packers kicked off, but Dallas failed to gain and Green Bay took possession of the ball on its 20-yard line.

Bart Starr barked his signals, took the snap from center Jim Ringo, spun around and handed off to Donny Anderson. Donny smashed through his own right tackle, picked up several yards, was hit hard by several Cowboys and fumbled the ball. But Chuck Mercein, tailing behind Anderson, alertly scooped up the loose ball and drove on for 5 more yards.

Utilizing the tremendous running power of Mercein and Donny Anderson, Starr kept the ball on the ground and the two Packer backs pounded the Dallas line for good yardage, running deep into Dallas territory.

Now the Packers were on the Dallas 8-yard line.

Starr took the snap from Ringo, started to roll out as if to pass the ball, then unexpectedly stopped in his tracks, wheeled and spotted Boyd Dowler in the end zone, and in the same easy, fluid motion, whipped a short pass to Boyd for a touchdown. Don Chandler kicked the extra point for the Packers, and midway in the first period, Green Bay jumped into the lead, 7–0.

Early in the second quarter, Bart Starr connected with a 46-yard pass to Dowler. The ball came floating into Dowler's outstretched arms as he fell over the goal line for another TD. Don Chandler's kick made it 14-0, Packers, and for the moment, it looked like Green Bay and Bart Starr—plus the zero weather—were going to be much too much for the Dallas Cowboys.

Now it was Dallas' turn, and the Cowboys quickly snapped off their first play—a long pass by Don Meredith—but with a great catch Herb Adderly of the Packers intercepted the ball and ran it to the Dallas 30-yard line. It looked like Green Bay was going to romp home an easy winner and their third straight NFL championship.

But suddenly, the Cowboys' defense stiffened. Bart Starr couldn't move the team on the ground. He rolled out for a pass and the Cowboys were all over him. Now it was fourth down and the Packers kicked to Dallas.

The failure to score after Adderly's interception seemed to affect the Packers. Suddenly the team seemed to lose its fine-honed precision, and its momentum came to a sudden halt. That's when Dallas started to come on. They became more aggressive, hit harder, blocked savagely, and slowly began to pierce the Packers' line for big yardage . . . and then a big break.

Bart Starr, deep in his own territory, faded back to pass. He never got rid of the ball. Willie Townes, the huge Dallas end was all over Bart . . . hit him hard and jarred the football from his hands. George Andrie, the Cowboys' fleet end, was right on the ball; scooping it up and dashing into the end zone for a touchdown.

The score was now 14–7, Green Bay, but seven points isn't much of a lead in a crucial football game, certainly not in a championship game.

The Cowboys were on the move now aroused by their first touchdown. They smashed into Green Bay's forward wall, driving into the secondary, shutting off the Packers' running game. Their aggressive play stopped Bart Starr before he could get the ball into the air. There were eight different occasions when Starr was smashed to the turf by the onrushing Dallas linemen as they simply overwhelmed the Packers' front wall.

Before the first half was over, another costly Green Bay fumble gave Dallas a chance to score again. Danny Villanueva kicked a field goal from the Green Bay 21-yard line to make the score, Green Bay, 14, Dallas, 10.

Bart Starr and his teammates weren't a happy bunch in the locker room between halves. The Packer defensive team had held the Cowboys, but two lapses on the part of the Packer offensive team had given Dallas 10 points. Another lapse in the Green Bay defense, another mistake by the offense, and the Cowboys could walk off the field winners, the dream of three straight National League Football championships gone forever.

And that very thing almost . . . happened.

For all that was on the line for the Packers, they couldn't develop an attack when they had possession of the ball. Twice, early in the third quarter, the Cowboys punched holes through the big Packer line and dumped Bart Starr for losses. Even when the Packer defense held, Starr couldn't find his receiver. The Packer receivers were finding it impossible to run their pass patterns on the icy gridiron.

Then, in the fourth quarter, with both teams playing tight defensive ball, and the Packers beginning to think that their 4-point edge might bring them victory, the Cowboys ran a play, which sent groans of despair through the packed stands of Packer backers.

Don Meredith, the brilliant quarterback of the Cowboys pulled a trick play out of his hat.

Don took the pass from his center and handed the ball to Dan Reeves. Reeves cut sharply to his left and the Packer cornerback, Bob Jeeter, moved in quickly to stop what looked like a dash off the left side of the line. It was a mistake.

Suddenly Reeves stopped dead in his tracks, whirled quickly, spotted his flying receiver, Lance Rentzel—who was all alone, uncovered, and some fifty yards downfield —and pitched a perfect pass to Rentzel. Lance gathered the ball in his arms and stepped over the goal line for 6 points. The play had covered more than 50 yards and Danny Villanueva's conversion made the score Dallas, 17, Green Bay, 14.

It looked like the end of the day for the Green Bay Packers and the finish of the dream Vince Lombardi had so much cherished: an unprecedented three straight National Football League championships.

But the most dramatic moment was yet to come, as the Packers drove and banged and clawed in a last-ditch effort to turn what looked like sure defeat into victory.

There were but five minutes left in the game. Green

Bay had the ball on its own 32-yard line. It was a long, long way to another touchdown, almost seventy yards.

Bart Starr, calm and almost detached, coolly started to move the Packers. His pin-point passes began to pick the Cowboys' defense apart. A Starr pass to Anderson was completed and Donny broke out into the clear and picked up 10 additional yards. Once again Bart took the pass from center Jim Ringo, faked a run to his left, whirled and deftly handed the ball off to Chuck Mercein, and Chuck, running as if his very life depended on this one mad dash, blasted aside at least three Cowboys defenders for 17 yards and another big first down.

Hope began to rise in the Green Bay squad as they fought and clawed for extra yardage on every play, and the huge, raucous Green Bay Packer fans were up on their feet roaring on every play.

Starr hit Boyd Dowler with another short pass, for another first down, and Green Bay was in Dallas territory.

"Go, Packers go! . . . Go Packers, Go!" they were yelling, screaming. Up on their feet chanting for their team.

The big stadium clock showed 1 minute 11 seconds to play.

And now Bart Starr called the key play of the game. He called a play the Packer offense had worked on all week. It was based on the Cowboys' Bob Lilly's aggressive line play, and Starr saved the strategy until he desperately needed the one big play of the year.

Lilly, a very quick, aggressive tackle for Dallas was continuously charging across the Packer line at the snap of the ball. He was giving Gale Gillingham, the Packer guard, trouble all afternoon, especially when Gale pulled out of the line to lead a play. Lilly would then charge through the hole left by Gale and grab the ball carrier from behind, for a loss. But this time Bart faked, giving the ball to Anderson, who was going to his right, and Gillingham pulled out and started to lead the play. Lilly then went through the hole after Anderson. But Starr, cleverly faking, handed the ball to Mercein. And Chuck blasted through the hole vacated by Lilly and went barreling down to the Dallas 3-yard line. It was a great call and a daring one by Starr.

There was less than a minute to play, less than 60 seconds, when Donny Anderson bulled his way to the Cowboys' 1-yard line, and a first down.

Anderson once more drove into the line, but this time the Cowboys rose en masse to stop him.

Twenty seconds left in the game. Twenty seconds.

Once more Donny Anderson was sent into the Dallas line for that precious 1 yard; but this time he slipped on the icy turf. Green Bay was now 1 foot away from the goal line and only 16 seconds before the final whistle.

Bart Starr looked to the side lines, to Vince Lombardi. Did the coach want to send Chandler in to try for the 3 points that would tie the game and send it into a sudden-death overtime period? Vincent Lombardi was a conservative coach. Bart Starr might have well expected Don Chandler to trot out on the field for the field goal. But Don Chandler was standing on the side lines, moving up and down on his feet, trying to keep from freezing. And Lombardi just shrugged his shoulders and pointed at Starr as if to say, "It's your game. You call the play."

It was all up to the quarterback. He was the one to make the fateful call. This was the last play of the game. Everybody on the field knew it. Everybody in the stands, frozen in the wind, their throats hoarse from exhorting their team to move across that Dallas goal line, knew it.

There was no time now for hesitation. A clock moves with extraordinary speed in those last few seconds of an exciting football game. If there had been time, Bart Starr might have thought of the days which brought him to stardom, and to this very great moment in his life, of his high school football days with Bobby Barnes and Nick Germanos, of his great success at Lanier High School and then the dismal years at the University of Alabama, and of the strange trick of fate that brought him together with the genius of Vince Lombardi; of his future and his hopes. But now, there was no time for thinking about anything but the precious strip of 12 inches of pay dirt, and how to get across that last wide chalk stripe, just a foot away from victory, and an unprecedented third straight NFL title.

Quickly in the huddle, Bart Starr called his own signal. He would take the ball in. He couldn't take a chance on a hand-off. He couldn't take a chance on any of his backs slipping. He would take complete responsibility. He would make it—or he would not.

The play called for Starr to slice in off his right guard's shoulder. In this play Bart was counting on Jerry Kramer to open the hole.

Starr barked off his signals, clutched the pass from center, Jim Ringo, cradled the ball in his arms and cracked through the tiny bit of daylight he saw. "Run to Daylight," Lombardi had preached, and Bart dove into the hole and was through and over the goal line.

Touchdown! The kick by Don Chandler. Green Bay, 21, Dallas, 17! The happy Green Bay players had to fight their way through the mob of hysterically happy rooters to get to their dressing rooms.

There were tears of joy in the locker room, and TV cameras and Vince Lombardi revealing for the first time that Bart Starr had played the entire game with bruised ribs, and a severe shoulder injury.

"To be a winner," said Vince Lombardi, "you've got to play even when you're hurt, and you've got to play to win."

Bryan Bartlett Starr, for that was the name he was given at birth, showed his teammates, the opposition, the whole football world, how to play when you're hurt, and how to win.

"Yes, sir," he said to the TV cameramen.

"No, sir," he said.

Modest, unassuming, he showed the sports world, too, that a "nice guy" can win.

"He is probably the best quarterback in football," said a coach of a rival club some few years before that 1967 championship game, "and before long he will be recognized as the greatest quarterback in professional football."

That afternoon, in 1967, winning the third consecutive National Football League championship, Bart Starr proved beyond all doubt that he was "the best of them all."

CHAPTER 2

Bryan Bartlett Starr was born in Montgomery, Alabama, January 9, 1934. Bryan was his father's middle name. Bartlett was the name of the doctor who ushered him into the world, the first man to slap him to life. Bryan Bartlett Starr can't remember the time anyone called him Bryan. Bartlett became Bart, and it was with the name of Bart Starr that he became known as one of the greatest stars in football's great constellation.

Benjamin Starr was stationed at the Alabama Air Corps base at the time of his son's arrival. Ben was an Army career man, a big, brawny man, a typical sergeant in the United States Armed Forces. He had been a boxer in his high school days, and he had the muscles to show for it. He had also played football when he had been at high school. He was a pretty fair baseball player, as well. With his high cheek bones, undoubtedly inherited from some distant forebear of his—some Cherokee Indian out of Oklahoma—Ben Starr was all athlete. And he passed on his interest and love for athletics and athletic competition to his two sons.

Bart was the first-born Starr. His brother, Hilton, was

born in 1936. Their father would have them both out on a field somewhere, whenever he had time for them or whenever he made time for them, pitching a baseball, showing both boys how to hit, batting the ball around, showing the boys how to throw a football.

"Touch or tackle?" asked Bart.

"You can tackle me," said the big, brawny Ben, "if you can. I'll do the touching."

The game would start with Ben and his two sons, but it grew fast enough, as other boys on the Army base joined in the fun. And it was fun, big Ben showing the boys how to throw the ball, how to catch it, how to make up plays and how to run them.

"My father was my first football coach," Bart Starr would tell anyone who asked him about his beginnings in football.

Ben Starr was a good coach for the Army youngsters, and a patient coach.

"I can't get a good grip on this ball," complained Bart. "My hands are too small."

"Don't worry about that, son," counseled the big sergeant, with the big hands. "Your hands will grow, just like you'll grow. Just make sure you grip the ball properly. Now, spread your fingers across the seam of the ball, and as you let the ball go forward step in the same direction with your left foot and throw. You'll be able to handle it all right."

"Hilton would have been a better player," Bart says, quietly, and there will be a touch of sadness in his eyes, as if he were remembering some profoundly unhappy moment of a time that was long, long ago.

Indeed it was an unhappy moment, the kind of moment that won't be forgotten, that stays with a man for as long as he lives. Hilton, like all kid brothers, tagged after his big brother Bart. And Bart, like all big brothers, gave his kid brother Hilton a rough time. Still, they were good pals and spent a lot of time with each other, playing ball and horsing around, particularly in the summertime, when they were both out of school.

One summer day, when Bart was twelve and Hilton ten, the two boys were playing hide-and-seek. They were barefoot. Hilton, looking for a good hiding place, running, stepped on a partly buried sharp bone, and the blood poured out of the deep gash in his foot. He was rushed to the hospital, given the usual shots against tetanus, but the shots didn't take. It was a freak accident. It was a freak, too, that the shots proved useless. He developed tetanus, and ten-year-old Hilton Starr, tragically, died.

"I missed him," Bart Starr still says. "There was suddenly a big empty space in my life. I know that I was only twelve years old at the time, but I don't think I've ever felt lonelier in all my life."

Bart Starr is a quiet man, a soft-spoken man, a self-effacing man, but he sounds convincing, in his soft Southern drawl, when he says, "Hilton had more natural athletic ability than I did. He had more fire in his play, too. My brother was the opposite of me. He was uninhibited—mean and nasty—and he would knock your block off with a tackle. I had to learn that. Hilton just did that naturally. That was the difference in our makeup. And I think my dad saw that. And I think it was the greatest thing he could have said to me. It got my fires going."

Ben Starr didn't quite agree with Bart's estimate of his brother Hilton's abilities, but he did say to Bart, on more than one occasion, "With your talent, if you had your brother Hilton's guts, you'd be able to make it anywhere."

"No, I've never forgotten Hilton," says Bart. "Many times I've thought of him in a tough game, and set myself, dedicated myself, to do something especially for my kid brother. Maybe it's hard to believe," he adds, "but I find myself doing just that, dedicating myself to some task for Hilton, even today."

Hilton's tragic death undoubtedly brought Bart and his father even closer than they had been before. Ben had only one son now, and like all fathers, he was ambitious for his son's career. That career, judging from Ben's interest and participation in sports, would be, most likely, a career in football or baseball—one of America's major sports.

"He never pushed me," says Bart. "He never said he wanted me to be a professional football player or a professional baseball player. We never even talked about a professional career in sports. I guess we just took it for granted."

Still, Ben Starr was out in the field somewhere, whenever he had or made a chance for it, to toss the ball around with his son and show him the finer points of football. And there can be no doubt that he encouraged Bart to try out for Montgomery's YMCA 100-pound football team.

It was with the Y team that Bart first joined the foot-ball wars, playing quarterback for the midget team. He didn't weigh much more than a hundred pounds when he played football for his junior high school team.

Bobby Barnes, now a successful automobile dealer in Montgomery, who is a life-long friend of Bart's, says that the first time he saw Bart in a football uniform he had a hard job to keep from laughing.

"There he was," says Barnes, who was to become a star football and baseball player for Alabama, as well as a star trackman, "a scrawny kid who couldn't have weighed more than a hundred and five or ten pounds, with a football uniform hanging loose all over him."

Bart Starr was a student at Baldwin Junior High School at that time. Bobby Barnes played for a rival school, Capital Heights Junior High School. The follow-ing year Bobby and Bart made the football squad at Sid-ney Lanier High School, the school named after a great American poet. Upon graduation, both Bobby Barnes and Bart Starr received scholarships to Alabama. But they met as rivals in the junior high school game.

"You know," says Barnes, "he was a tough little com-petitor even then. He didn't have the tools, not yet, but playing against him I knew he had plenty of football sense. Maybe that's what drew me to him. I liked him, even in that suit that flopped all over him."

There were other reasons that brought these two young athletes together. They were both quiet boys. Nei-ther one of them talked too much.

And "his mamma used to make the best pound cake I ever ate."

"By the way," Bobby Barnes will tell anyone, coming out of nowhere, "some people say Bart Starr can't run. Well let me tell you, he could have made the track team anywhere."

And with no encouragement at all, Bobby Barnes will go on to prove his point.

"Have you ever been on a bird shoot?" he will ask.

He won't wait for an answer.

"Well, Bart and I cut our sixth period class at Lanier High School one day, and went on a bird shoot.

"We got into this cornfield, with our shotguns, where we had spotted some birds. We didn't know whose cornfield it was, and for a while we didn't care.

"Then Bart spotted a truck coming down the road and we knew the farmer wasn't going to like our stomping in his cornfield, so we took off. We moved fast, jumping ditches and all that sort of thing, and I was supposed to be fast. I was the fastest man on the Lanier High School track team. But you should have seen Bart.

"Here I was, running as fast as I could; and there was Bart, catching up with me, and passing me like a shot. I tell you, that Bart Starr can run. He can run with the best of them."

Bart's reputation at the junior high school, however, didn't seem to carry any weight with Bill Mosely, the football coach at Sidney Lanier High School.

"He was one of those silent boys out for the team," said Mosely, "but that first year of high school he was kind of small for the team and there was nothing about him that made me pay him any special attention."

That first year at Lanier Bart sat on the bench. He

was a bench warmer, and he felt miserable about it. Lanier had a tough football schedule, playing some of the best high schools in the region. Starr felt that he was neglected because of his rather small size. The only times Bart got into a game was when the battle on the gridiron had been all but won, or hopelessly lost.

"Bart Starr was alert," admitted Coach Mosely. "He was a good listener and he had a good head. All I ever noticed about him in that first year was his alertness, and quiet, positive attitude. I never had to explain a play twice to Bart. He didn't fool around when he was out there playing the game or practicing for it. He was all business. I never doubted for a minute that he was always out there, trying. He was on the field to make the team, to play football."

Those were kind statements that Coach Mosely made, and they were an accurate enough appraisal of Bart Starr. But nothing seemed to convince the coach that the young football player would be more helpful on the field than on the bench. Bart's freshman year at Sidney Lanier was full of misery and unhappiness, even discouragement.

"I'm quitting," he said to his father after a frustrating afternoon of practice. "I can't make the first team. Coach Mosely doesn't think I'm even good enough for the traveling team."

"O.K.," said Ben, seemingly unruffled. "That'll give you time to cut down some corn stalks. You can turn the earth, too. Get it ready for spring planting."

"Yes, sir," said Bart, but he never did get to cutting the corn stalks or turning the earth.

"I hated gardening," he says, "so I just went back to football practice and warming the bench for Coach Mosely." It was a good move, and fate helped make it a good move.

As Coach Mosely said, Bart Starr was all business on the gridiron. He went out on the field to work. And he worked. He asked questions, and he studied his play book every day. Maybe nobody ever told him, but he knew that practice, practice, and more practice made the ballplayer.

"Forget about passing," his friends would say, as he tried to grip the pigskin with his still small hands. But Bart paid no attention and continued to practice his passing, and his practicing paid off.

CHAPTER 3

Bart Starr shouted out his encouragement to his teammates as the Lanier High School football team trotted
on to the field to await the opening kickoff for the third
game of the 1950 season—a game against Tuscaloosa,
one of the strongest teams, one of the mightiest football
powers in the state of Alabama. Tuscaloosa, led by its
all-star tackle, Hugh Thomas, son of Alabama's famous
coach, Frank Thomas, was undefeated in seventeen consecutive games, and a crowd of more than 12,000 football fans had turned out for the game at Montgomery's
Cramton Field.

Bart had done his level best during preseason practice
to earn a starting position as quarterback, but he was up
against the brilliant veteran, Don Shannon, and Shannon wasn't about ready to relinquish his position. Don
was a fine passer, a fast and shifty runner, and a cool,
resourceful team leader; and under his direction Lanier
High had previously beaten Alex City High School,
33–0, and Douthan High, 14–7.

So, Bart sat on the bench with the rest of the substi-
tutes as he watched Shannon, Bobby Barnes, Don Aber-

nathy, and Jimmy Moore run brilliantly against Tuscaloosa.

There was a sudden break in the hard-hitting action as Don Shannon was tackled hard by a horde of Tuscaloosa linemen and he lay where he was hit. On the ground, unable to move and in great pain.

The crowd of more than 12,000 were silent as they carried the fine young quarterback off the field on a stretcher. His leg was broken.

Coach Mosely looked over to his bench, sighed with dismay, and shook his head. This game against Tuscaloosa, the biggest game of the year, might actually decide the state championship. But how could he possibly delude himself into thinking about the championship without his star quarterback? How could Lanier stand any kind of a chance with a skinny, 150 pound, inexperienced, sixteen-year-old substitute?

"Bart," he shouted. "Bart Starr, over here."

Bart excitedly dashed to the coach's side as Mosely continued. "Now look, son. This is your chance. Don't take any unnecessary chances. Play straight conservative football. Nothing fancy, O.K.?"

"Yes, sir, Coach. Nothing but straight football. Yes sir," and Bart raced out onto the field as the crowd suddenly stirred and began to shout his name.

Bart quickly called his team into a huddle. His hands were suddenly wet with sweat. Butterflies danced around in his stomach. He had been working, waiting, praying for two years for this chance to show Coach Mosely what he could do. Now, suddenly his nerves were at loose ends.

He was greatly concerned about Don Shannon. He hoped that he hadn't been hurt too badly. For a moment, too, he wondered whether he was as good as he thought he was, but only for a moment. Now there wasn't time to think about Shannon. He had to take charge of the team and he had to show his teammates that he could do the job.

In the huddle his first problem arose.

"Bart, let's surprise 'em with a quick down and out," said end Nick Germano. "I know I can beat my man."

"No, let's move on the ground. We've got 'em going," said Don Abernathy. "We've been doing O.K. on the ground. Let's keep the offense moving."

"Now, all you guys stop that jabbering," said Starr. His voice was sharp and to the point. "I'm the guy in charge in the huddle. I'll call all the plays. When I want your advice, I'll ask. Just you guys do your job from now on. Is that clear?"

Bart looked around at the faces of his teammates as he curtly called . . . "47 on 3 . . . to the right." The players moved out of the huddle and quickly lined up into their offensive positions.

Then sharply, Bart's strong voice cut the air:

"Hut 15 . . . 37 . . . 47." The ball came back to Bart. He faked a hand-off, rolled out to his right, stopped suddenly, looked left and pitched a perfect pass to halfback Bobby Barnes, who was streaking down the sidelines. Bobby caught the pass and was knocked out of bounds. The play was good for a first down.

Once again, in the huddle, Bart called another play and the players quickly responded. This time Bart took the ball from his center, captain John Snoderly, handed it to Don Abernathy, and Don blasted through the line for 8 more yards.

And now, suddenly the big crowd came to life and roared, "Starr, Starr, Let's go Bart Starr."

Now, suddenly the entire Lanier squad was on fire. They were responding to Bart's firm leadership and they surged forward on every play, driving their opponents into the ground.

Coach Bill Mosely could hardly believe his eyes. There was this young quarterback—only sixteen years old, weighing no more than 150 pounds and without any varsity experience—running the team as if he had been doing it all his life.

After a seesaw first half in which neither team could score, Bart started the third period by calling a complicated play. He took the snap from his center and faked a hand-off to Bobby Barnes, then whirled and lateraled the ball to Don Abernathy. Don immediately tossed a long pass to Herb Gay. Gay caught the ball for a gain of more than 25 yards and the big crowd whooped it up once again. On the next play, Bart passed to left end, Ulmer Priester, for another first down and Lanier began to move once more.

Don Abernathy plowed through his own right guard, picked up some fine blocking, broke through the Tuscaloosa secondary, and raced to the Tuscaloosa 5-yard line before he was brought down. Bart Starr carried the ball on the very next play, and swept into the end zone for the touchdown. Larry Hayes's kick for the extra point was wide. Score, 6–0.

In the final quarter, Bart kept the big Tuscaloosa line off balance as he cleverly mixed a superb passing game with some fine running, as the Lanier team drove on to the goal line.

With the ball on the Tuscaloosa 38-yard line, speedy Bobby Barnes, who had performed spectacularly all afternoon, took a shovel pass from Starr and raced into the end zone for another Lanier score. This time Larry Hayes's kick was good and Lanier had upset the strongest team in the state to win, 13–0.

Coach Mosely was the first to reach Bart as the final whistle sounded. He grabbed the youngster's hand, pumped it vigorously and said, "Bart, I'm proud of you today. Matter of fact, I just can't believe the kind of job you and the rest of the boys did. I'm proud of all you fellas." And then the more than one thousand happy Lanier students rushed, pummeled, and congratulated Bart, Bobby Barnes, and the rest of the players on their tremendous upset victory over a Tuscaloosa squad that had previously won seventeen straight games.

The very next day Coach Mosely called Bart into his office and handed him a batch of papers.

"These are the plays we're going to use for the rest of the schedule. Now, Bart, I want you to study these plays. I want you to memorize them so you will know your own pattern on each play, and as the quarterback, you'll have to know the job every man does on each play. We'll go over each play sheet tomorrow. We'll discuss them, talk about them. If you have questions, don't hesitate to ask. Then, when you've fully digested all this material, we'll get out on the field and go through each and every step, of every play. I'll diagram the position of each player, so that you can give me the answer to any play situation . . . at any time."

When he was through with his discourse, Coach Mosely stood up, walked over to Bart, put his arm around him and said,

"Bart, I've seen a lot of men and boys play this game of football. A lot of big men, good men, great players in college and in the professional ranks. But you've got something a lot of those fellas never had. You've got a sixth sense for this game that will make you a fine quarterback, and perhaps some day a fine coach. Now, go on home and work on these plays."

Three days later, Bart had mastered the plays.

"Explain them to me," said the coach. "I want to know where every man on the team moves. I want to know who blocks, who carries the ball, every assignment."

Studiously and carefully, Bart detailed the entire program of plays. He explained the movement of every man, on every play. His report was clear, concise, and correct. The coach couldn't have been more pleased.

"Now, we may yet have a winning season," he said.

"Bart Starr was the kind of player I could plan and develop an entire offensive system around. I created an entire series of new plays to take advantage of Bart's particular abilities. He was that good. In fact, he was the smartest young football player, the greatest passer I've ever seen play high school football."

CHAPTER 4

The big college football scouts had noted the play of several members of the Lanier High School team, had filed reports on the spectacular Bart Starr, the sensational break-away sprinting of Bobby Barnes, and the great pass-catching end, Nick Germanos. They singled out Starr in their reports, noting his accurate passing, amazing punting, deliberate, team leadership, and the scholarship offers came pouring in.

If Bart was outstanding in his junior year, he was truly spectacular in 1951, his senior year. In recognition of his outstanding play, Bart was elected captain of the Lanier eleven. He was happy too, that Bobby Barnes, his best friend was elected co-captain, and the two friends, delighted at the honor, were determined that 1951 would be a championship year.

Throughout the spring and summer, Bart and Bobby talked football, practiced their skills, sharpened their passing attack. Of course both boys worked at odd jobs to earn some extra money, but even during working hours all the talk was football, and the extra work paid off in dividends as the co-captains led Sidney Lanier High School to one of its finest records.

In the opening game of the season against Alex City High, Starr directed the team in masterly fashion and Barnes dashed for two touchdowns as Lanier easily won, 12–0. The following week Dothan High was defeated 20–7, for the team's thirteenth consecutive victory, during a two-year span.

In the annual game against Tuscaloosa, Bart was nothing less than spectacular as he completed 7 out of 9 passes and scored a touchdown on a pass roll-out play. He tossed a sparkling 35-yard pass to end Nick Germanos for a second TD, then in succession threw 5 straight passes to Germanos and Barnes, and whipped a 25-yarder to Eddie Reeder for a third touchdown. Final score, Lanier, 21, Tuscaloosa, 6.

The following week, Lanier suffered its first defeat in two years bowing to a heavier, more experienced Ramsey High squad, 26–6. However, the next week, Starr and Barnes rallied the team, spurred them on to successive victories over Phoenix City High School, 26–4, and a stunning upset over Murphy High, 19–13, in a game marked by Starr's passing; he completed 11 out of 12 passes, while Bobby Barnes thrilled a crowd of more than 12,000 fans with a brilliant 95-yard touchdown sprint that clinched the win for Lanier.

Late in November, Lanier High traveled north to play one of Kentucky's leading teams, Louisville's Manual High. Once more the college scouts from all over the nation were in the stands. Watching with their binoculars, they wanted to see once again, if this young Bart

Starr, talked about so much all over Alabama, would fold up against the pressure pass rush of Manual's big line.

Early in the first quarter Bart faded back to pass. A wave of Manual tacklers charged at him. Bart slipped past one lineman's grasp and dashed for the side lines, the hard-charging lineman at his heels. Bart ignored them, while he searched the field for his receivers. A lineman grabbed his arm, Bart twisted away, another rushed him, Bart ducked, and the tackler fell down. Then, as calm as if he were watching a parade, Bart straightened out, cocked his arm back, and snapped off a 25-yard TD pass to his favorite receiver, Nick Germanos.

And high up in the stands the coaches and the scouts knew how this young Bart Starr from Alabama would stand up when under great pressure.

Slowly, carefully, and thoughtfully, Starr maneuvered the Lanier team downfield against the heavier Manual team. Lanier drove for another touchdown. And up in the stands the coaches shook their heads. One said to another, "I've got to get that boy for my school."

"I don't know," said another. "But you're going to have to beat me out. I want him for my school."

And then the two scouts, followed by an array of coaches raced down the stairs to talk to Starr in the locker room.

CHAPTER 5

Bart Starr had been offered football scholarships by over a dozen schools. He might have elected to go to one of the big campuses in California or one of the better schools in the East. He might have chosen one of the football colleges in Florida or one of the Big Ten, with all the publicity playing for a Big Ten eleven promised. But, for a while anyway, Starr was set on going to the University of Kentucky, where the great "Bear" Bryant was head coach.

Bart had been invited by the "Bear" to visit the school. He had been ushered around the beautiful Kentucky campus by the head coach. The "Bear" had sequestered himself with the young quarterback and had gone into details with him on the Kentucky Wildcats' strategy and tactics on the gridiron, and made him feel welcome.

It was all fascinating to the young quarterback from Montgomery, Alabama. Always shy, Bart may have been a bit discomforted by all the attention showered on him by the legendary coach. But this was the manner in which many college coaches secured the much-needed talent each year. Bart lost himself in the details of Kentucky's offensive and defensive play, and he liked the idea that Bear Bryant, one of the nation's great coaches, talked about developing a set of plays to fit Bart's style.

Of course, it was flattering to have Bear Bryant spend so much time with him. But what sold him solidly, for the time being anyway, on Kentucky, was his meeting with Babe Parilli.

Babe Parilli was Kentucky's star quarterback. He was an All-American quarterback. He must have been the idol of almost every high school quarterback in the country. He certainly was Bart Starr's idol.

"I hope you're coming to Kentucky?" Parilli asked Bart.

There was only one answer Starr could give to that question.

Babe Parilli, his idol, had shaken his hand. He could still feel the strength of it in his own fingers. Kids always dream of meeting their idols. Bart Starr's kid dream had come true. He had met, talked with, and shaken hands with one of the nation's great football stars.

"If Kentucky will have me," said Bart.

"Sure we'll have you," said Parilli. "We'd like you up here. We can use you."

"Thank you, sir," said the young Starr.

It was the life in the Army camp, with his top-sergeant father, Ben Starr, which had inculcated Bart with a sense of respect for rank. It was always "Yes, sir" and "No, sir," when Bart spoke to his teachers, his coaches, his elders. But it was—and still is—"Yes, sir" and "No, sir" to anyone, regardless of that person's rank or station. Bart was naturally polite, courteous, and soft spoken. "Thank you, sir," said Bart to his idol, Babe Parilli.

He thought, but didn't dare say at the moment, "Some day, like you Mr. Parilli, I'd like to be the Number One quarterback for the University of Kentucky; and maybe All-American, too." But that is exactly what occupied Bart Starr in his last few weeks at Lanier High School in Montgomery.

"What college are you going to?" his pals would ask him.

"Kentucky, I think," Bart would answer. "If Coach Bryant will have me there."

"Why not Alabama?" asked Bobby Barnes. "I'm going there, and so is Germanos. Couple of the other boys are gonna enroll. Going there to play football and baseball. Say Bart, if you change your mind, and I sure hope you do, it'll be the old Lanier passing and running combination. Starr to Barnes to Germanos."

"I've really thought about it," Bart would say.

And he had thought about it. He had thought a great deal about Alabama.

The Crimson Tide of Alabama had a great reputation and had well earned it in its gridiron wars. In 1926 the Tide traveled to the Rose Bowl to defeat the highly touted squad from the University of Washington. In 1927 Alabama again traveled to the Rose Bowl to battle the great Stanford eleven to a 7–7 tie. In 1931 they vanquished Washington State, 24–0, in their third Rose

Bowl appearance; and in 1935 the Tide walloped Stanford 29–13 in a fourth Rose Bowl game.

Alabama had a formidable football team, as well as a national reputation. It was a college any young athlete would dream of joining in its athletic accomplishments. Alabama had offered Bart Starr a scholarship. It was indeed an honor to be invited to become part of that legendary Crimson Tide, and Bart was pleased and flattered by Alabama's invitation.

Still, there was Bear Bryant at Kentucky and, even more enticing, there was Babe Parilli.

"I'm going to Kentucky," said Bart Starr.

But he didn't.

There was one factor Bart had failed for a time to consider. It was the romantic factor. For, indeed, there was a girl in Bart's life, a very pretty girl. It was the girl who was to make young Starr, almost at the last minute, change his mind about the college he would play football for.

"Bart wasn't one to talk very much," says his old school pal, Bobby Barnes, "but he was just one of the boys whenever we got together. Girls? Now that's something different. I never knew anyone who was as shy as Bart around the girls. He'd duck his head just to keep from speaking to them, even if it were only to say, "Good morning." He never went out with a girl when we were at school, not until he met Cherry Morton."

Bart had had his eye on Cherry Morton for a long time. She was an exceedingly attractive young lady. He'd remark to his pal, Bobby Barnes, from time to time, on how pretty she was.

"Why don't you ask her for a date?" asked Barnes.

Bart just looked at Bobby, and maybe he blushed a little, but he never had the courage to speak to Cherry, not at that time anyway. Curiously enough, Cherry was as shy as Bart and, however much she might have been attracted by the young football star, they never would have had that date, if it hadn't been for the initiative of Bobby and his girl friend, Norma Hedrick.

It was Bobby and Norma who arranged for the first meeting between Bart Starr and Cherry Morton. They double-dated the first time when the Lanier football squad went to play that memorable game against Kentucky. After that, it was double-date all the time.

It had taken a long time for Bart to be attracted by a young lady, but once attracted, it was to prove something that was going to last forever.

Cherry, as well as Bart, was about to graduate from Sidney Lanier High School in Montgomery. Cherry had already made her college choice, but she didn't want to influence Bart's decision. When she at last thought that Bart had made up his mind firmly—that there was no doubt about his going to Kentucky—Cherry announced that she was going to Auburn, in Alabama.

"Wait a minute," said Bart. "You're going to Auburn and I'm going to Kentucky?"

"I suppose so," said Cherry.

"But Auburn and Kentucky are a long way from each other," protested Bart. "How are we going to see each other?"

"It won't be easy, I guess," said Cherry.

"No," confirmed Bart. "And suppose you meet some other fellow?"

"You know I won't be going out with some other fellow," said Cherry.

"Maybe not," said Bart.

He wasn't sure. He didn't want to lose Cherry.

"I could go to Alabama," he said. "That would be closer to you."

"You go where you want to go," said Cherry. "I don't want you to change your mind because of me."

But that is exactly what Bart Starr did. Cherry was more important to him than Kentucky, more important to him than anything else in his young world.

"I'm going to Alabama," he said.

And much to the disappointment of Bear Bryant and the University of Kentucky, but much to the delight of Red Drew, coach of the Crimson Tide, and the rest of the college, Bart Starr enrolled at the University of Alabama.

Bart enrolled at Alabama to be closer to Cherry, but the University of Alabama was to prove a terribly disappointing experience—one that might have shattered for all time the future career of one of America's great football heroes.

CHAPTER 6

Bart Starr enrolled at the University of Alabama in 1952. The Korean War draft had depleted the ranks of the athletic squads in the colleges and had brought about an unusual N.C.A.A. ruling. For the duration of the war, freshmen, who had heretofore been barred from playing varsity ball, were permitted to participate in the varsity program, at the discretion of the coaches.

The ruling proved to be a break for Red Drew, coach of the Crimson Tide, and for Bart Starr as well. The eighteen-year-old youngster wasn't quite ready to take over the Number One quarterback spot, but Red Drew had him playing in the very first game of the season, against Mississippi Southern. If Bart was nervous, as he very well might have been, playing his first big college game, no one noticed. On the contrary, from the moment he stepped on to that gridiron, Drew, his coaching staff, and all the Alabama fans knew they had a winner.

"Opportunity knocks but once," wrote the sports reporter for the University's weekly paper, *The Crimson-White*, "and Bart Starr, freshman, was not one to fail in opening the door."

Following the third game of the season, against Virginia Tech, *The Crimson-White* reporter devoted two columns to the new quarterback out of Montgomery.

"In the Mississippi Southern game," wrote the sportswriter, "Bart Starr proved himself an able quarterback, handling the ball with clock-like precision. The Virginia Tech game proved his worth was not by chance. For the two games his passing percentage is 66⅔ per cent, completing 8 out of 12 attempts.

"Bart is 18 years old and weighs 170 pounds. He wrapped up All-City honors twice, and he was All-American in his senior year at Lanier High School. It seems that Bart is all that his last name implies, Star.

"Bart's girl goes to Auburn. Bart says she will root for us when we play Auburn." Then, quoting Bart, "She'd better!"

The sports editor of *The Crimson-White* went his reporter one better.

"Alabama football players who should know what they are talking about," he wrote, "are saying that frosh QB whiz Bart Starr is potentially another Gilmer."

Gilmer was Harry Gilmer, perhaps the greatest of the Alabama gridders ever named All-American, a legend on the campus of the Crimson Tide.

Bart didn't play in every game of Alabama's football schedule that freshman year. The Crimson Tide had a rugged schedule: Mississippi State, Georgia, Georgia Tech, Tennessee, among others. But Bart got into enough games and had more than enough playing time to earn his first Varsity Letter. Coach Red Drew saw fit, too, to send his freshman quarterback into the Orange

Bowl game against the vaunted eleven from Syracuse. And Bart's performance that afternoon sent the Alabama rooters completely berserk.

It didn't matter that the Crimson Tide had rolled over the Syracuse squad. It didn't matter that it was late in the game which had already been won by the Alabama eleven. Bart Starr trotted onto the field and did exactly what he had to do—and magnificently.

The ball was on the Alabama 7-yard line when Bart took over the chores as Alabama's quarterback. The crowd of some 81,500 roaring fans did not faze him, nor did the fact that he had never played in a game of such national significance. He calmly took over and immediately took to the air for his first play.

Bart threw 12 passes, completing 8 of them. The eighth time, Bart whipped a 30-yard pass to Bobby Marlow, who dashed into the end zone. Touchdown!

The crowd filled the huge Orange Bowl with a mighty roar. Bart Starr just turned and, head down, in his typical modest fashion, ran off the field, so that the kicker could come in to try for that extra point.

"Look at him!" shouted an Alabama fan. "Did you ever see anything like it? A freshman! He throws a touchdown! And he runs off the field like he's done nothing at all!"

The fans, in years to come, would see this scene repeated, one way or another, on the professional gridiron.

"Cool!" they would say, with admiration.

"He just doesn't know how good he is!"

"How can a man do all he does with the football and still keep his hat size?"

Modesty. That was the answer in that Bowl game, when he was a freshman. That would be the answer so long as Bart Starr played football—college football or professional football. On the playing field or off it, Bart Starr was and is possessed of that virtue which is so uncommon among us, humility.

Bart Starr started the season as Alabama's Number One quarterback for the Crimson Tide in 1953. It was a great year for Alabama. It was a great year for the sophomore from Montgomery.

Of the 11 games in which the nineteen-year-old quarterback led the Tide, Alabama won 6, tied 2 and lost 2, to win the sectional division championship and go on to play against Rice in the Cotton Bowl. Against Rice, Bart was the defensive star of the day, intercepting 3 passes and playing an outstanding game.

For Bart Starr, the season of 1953 proved to be an almost unprecedented triumph.

Harry Gilmer, the All-American Alabama hero, had passed the ball for 930 yards in 1945, his best season at the school. Bart had missed one game, because of injuries, yet his passing was good for 870 yards. He had 59 completions out of 119 attempts, for an approximately 50 per cent average. Eight of his passes were good for touchdowns, a record in the Southeastern Football Conference.

"He's the greatest passer in the history of Alabama football," was the universal opinion on the campus of the Crimson Tide.

"Greater than Harry Gilmer?"

"Greater than Harry Gilmer!"

In addition, Coach Red Drew discovered that Bart was one of the finest punters in the nation. It was a discovery that wasn't going to help the young fellow's career at Alabama. Bart did kick for an average of 41 yards. He was the second best college punter in the United States, but he paid for his kicking ability. One of those kicking attempts was going to put him out of action and put a damper on what certainly looked like a most promising career on the gridiron.

It was in August of the following year, 1954, that Bart Starr's promising football career was suddenly brought to an excruciating stop. He was practicing his kicking. He had always been sold on the value of practice and, till that day, his practicing had paid off. He was always among the first on the field and among the very last to leave. It was never too early for him to begin football practice for the coming season. Kicking had become one of his duties now for the Crimson Tide, and there wasn't enough time in the day for practice. He worked on his passing, and when everyone else was through practicing, Bart would work on his kicking.

That day in August 1954 he was working on his kicking game, practicing those long booming punts, angling the ball to the side lines.

"Good kick!" said the player working out with him on the field.

"Not enough height," said Bart.

"That wasn't too bad," came back his companion.

"More height," insisted Bart.

He got the ball again. He put his foot into it. There was the distance again, and this time, good height, but Bart wasn't watching. He had felt a strange pop in his back, a sharp twinge.

"Something wrong?" asked his companion, seeing the pain in Bart's eyes.

"Nothing," said Bart, trying to shake off the definite ache in his back. "Let me have the ball."

He kicked the ball again, and this time there was no concealing the pain he felt in his back.

"Maybe you ought to quit for a while," suggested the player practicing with Bart.

"No. It's nothing," said Bart. "It'll go away."

He picked up the ball and tried another punt, but this time he could not lift his foot. The pain was awful.

"I guess you're right," he said to his friend. "Maybe I ought to take it easy for a while."

Bart would have to take it easy, all right. He would have to take it easy for a long time.

He tried to throw a pass the next day. It was no good. He couldn't get the proper speed into the pass. He couldn't hit his target. He was short. That pain in his back was crippling. He couldn't get any distance, and the accuracy for which he had been so heralded in 1953 was all but gone.

It got so that it became painful just to grip the football.

"I think I'd better see somebody about this," he said.

The "somebody" was the doctor, who took X rays, then gave Bart the bad news.

"It's the sacroiliac. You've thrown it out," said the doctor.

"What can I do for it?" asked Bart.

"Rest," said the doctor.

"You mean that I can't play football?" queried the worried youngster.

"I wouldn't think so," said the doctor. "It's going to hurt every time you move. The more you move the more it will hurt."

"And rest is the only thing that'll cure it?"

The doctor nodded his head. "While you're resting, I might put you in traction. That might help a great deal. We'll see."

There are only four years of football at college. Bart wasn't going to give up one of those years easily.

He was out on the field again, trying to toss the ball, trying to pass it, but the pain got worse and worse. It got so that Bart could hardly lift his arms.

"The doctor is right," he finally admitted and much of that 1954 season, Alabama's star quarterback spent lying in traction in a bed in the campus hospital.

Yet, there were days when the pain was just a bit less severe, and Bart did manage to get into a few games for the Crimson Tide; not enough to make it a winning season for Alabama, but long enough to connect with 24 of 41 attempted passes.

It was a disappointing year for the University of Alabama. It was a bitterly frustrating year for Bart Starr. But 1955, Bart's senior year, was to prove even more disastrous.

Red Drew resigned his coaching post with the Crimson Tide after the failure of the 1954 season. He was replaced by J. B. ("Ears") Whitworth. Whitworth had been a linesman on Alabama's great teams of 1930 and 1931. He had kicked a field goal in the 1931 Rose Bowl pasting of Washington State. He had stayed on as an assitant coach at Alabama and had been an assistant coach with Louisiana State and Georgia, then signed on as head coach at Oklahoma A & M. He still had a year to go with the Oklahoma Aggies, but they were quite willing to let him go. His record with the Aggies had been far from satisfactory. It was off a losing season that he came to his alma mater. He came full of promise and hope for his old University, but he wasn't going to deliver.

"I look for Alabama to come back mighty fast," he announced on entering the campus.

It was J. B. Whitworth's opinion that the senior gridders at Alabama had developed the losing habit.

"They've grown accustomed to losing," he said. "It was a losing team last year, and they probably think they're going to be a losing team this year."

It was a curious kind of logic, particularly for a man who had played for the Crimson Tide and knew the spirit of the men who played for Alabama. Still it was his logic and he accepted his logic as something infallible.

"We're going to start the season," he announced, "with a squad of sophomores and juniors."

It was almost unbelievable, but those responsible for hiring Whitworth had to go along with the new coach's decision and hope for the best. Whitworth had his way.

Bart and all the other seniors, veterans of the 1954 gridiron wars, sat on the bench through most of the game as
Rice walloped the Crimson Tide in the first game of
what would develop into Alabama's worst gridiron record
in all its years of football. The score was 20–0.

In the second game of the Tide's '55 schedule,
Vanderbilt defeated Alabama 21-6. T.C.U. ran over them
21–0. Tennessee almost duplicated the score, 20–0. And
so it went, with the man who had been Alabama's brilliant sophomore quarterback, Bart Starr, warming the
Tide's bench.

The only time Coach Whitworth sent any of his seniors into the game, including Bart Starr, was when a
game had been hopelessly lost.

"It was depressing," says Bart. "I began to lose
confidence in myself."

When Coach Whitworth did give him a call, Starr
couldn't get that feeling of command, couldn't get the
proper drive, the adrenal push, all so necessary for the
aggressive gridder.

"When I'd get out there on the field," Bart says, "I
just wasn't the kind of quarterback I should have been,
the kind of leader I'd been as a junior, a sophomore, a
freshman."

Even so, in the short period of time he played Bart
threw 96 passes, 55 of them right on the target, for a
better than 56 per cent average. It was an average that
should have given his coach second thoughts on his
game plans. But it didn't. Every time Bart was inserted
into a game, the Tide seemed to come alive, gained
ground, and began to look like a winning football team.

1. Bart Starr, age fourteen, shows his excellent punting form.

2. Don Shannon (left) and Bart Starr—the Lanier High
School quarterback rivals. (*Albert Kraus Photo*)

3. Joe Rodgers and Bart study some plays with Lanier coach Bill Moseley.

4. Starr (rear, right) played in a high school All-Star game.

5. The quarterback from the University of Alabama. (*Yeatman King Photo*)

It was Starr's fine passing and running in the final quarter of the game against Georgia Tech that finally put Alabama on the scoreboards as Tech routed Alabama 35–14. That, however, seemed to make little impression on the coach, and Whitworth continued his policy of utilizing only sophomores and freshmen; and Bart Starr was forced to just sit on the bench while 'Bama went through the worst season in its football history, losing all ten—every game—on its 1955 schedule.

It was a miserable year for twenty-year-old Bart Starr. For most of those twenty years he had known only success—blinding, brilliant success. He had been a sensational high school quarterback, an All-American nominee; a crack baseball and basketball player. In the classroom he learned quickly and easily and was near the head of his class. He had accepted success with a cool poise. He never bragged. He never exulted over a defeated opponent.

Now he would know six long years of failure, the ashen taste of defeat nearly always in his mouth. He would learn what it is like to be a loser on a team of losers.

Bart Starr did not accept being a loser. It hurt him like the sting of an open wound. He was most unhappy. Sometimes he wondered if he weren't chasing after something he couldn't ever catch, like a small boy chasing a butterfly.

But through all the losing, Bart Starr was never the sore loser. He never whined to teammates that he wasn't getting a fair chance. He never sulked in practice. He never threw up his hands and said, "I am quitting."

In defeat, at least on the surface, he was always the poised young man. Inside he burned, raging to prove himself. But rarely did he let that rage shatter his calmness.

"I wanted to play pro ball," said Bart. "Secretly hoped that one of the pro scouts had noticed me, would draft me. But since I didn't play very much those last two years, I kind of lost hope."

But, for a moment, there was a ray of hope for Bart. He was selected to play in the annual post-season Blue and Gray Game in early January, and he played a marvelous defensive game. His play was of such quality, that Coach Charley Winner of the Baltimore Colts approached him and asked if he would be willing to play on the defense for the Colts.

"I'll play anywhere, coach," Bart said.

But Winner never contacted Bart again, and so Bart thought, "there goes my last opportunity."

CHAPTER 7

Johnny Dee, a former great Notre Dame star, was the basketball coach at Alabama. He had watched the Crimson Tide football squad through its dismal 1955 losing season with something bordering on disbelief.

"Why doesn't Whitworth use Starr?" he muttered to himself.

It wasn't ethical for one coach to criticize a coach of another sport. Dee knew an outstanding athlete when he saw one. He had watched Bart's progress as a freshman, sophomore, junior and senior; he liked and admired the courage and poise of the young quarterback and had befriended him. Dee admired a smart ballplayer and told Bart that he had a future as a pro-football player because of these attributes. He also knew that the big professional football scouts were not checking Alabama—after all the team had lost every game on its schedule.

Johnny Dee didn't like talent going to waste. He certainly wasn't going to let Bart Starr go to waste. He sat down and wrote a letter to one of his good friends, Jack Vanisi. Vanisi was the business manager of the Green Bay Packers.

He wrote, "Jack, you don't want to miss Bart Starr in your draft. He's got all the essentials and would make a fine quarterback. He's a great passer, a fine kicker, and commands respect from all of his teammates. He's also a very bright young man, an A student. I think he would be a fine Green Bay Quarterback prospect."

The Green Bay Packers were destined to become one of the truly great teams in all of professional football, but in 1955 they were in sorry shape. The team, needing badly to rebuild, was looking for young football players.

Johnny knew, too, that Green Bay wasn't the most attractive spot on the professional football map. The players called it "Siberia," and for a couple of reasons. First, it was the squad itself, a consistent group of losers. Second, Green Bay was a cold town, the coldest spot in the football circuit, so far as the weather went. Besides, Green Bay was a small town. There was little a man could do in Green Bay, if he wasn't playing football. It possessed little of the glamour a player could look forward to in any of the bigger towns and cities.

Coach Johnny Dee knew all this, but he also knew that there was little chance for Bart Starr to be drafted by any of the big glamorous teams; not because of Bart's lack of ability, but just because they didn't know him. Green Bay, he felt, wisely enough, might be hungry enough to draft any good quarterback prospect.

In Green Bay, Jack Vanisi received Johnny Dee's letter, read it, then forgot about it. When the drafting for the 1956 football season began, Bart Starr was nowhere near his mind.

Drafting is a long and sometimes tedious procedure. The most desirable prospects are drafted immediately. For the rest, it becomes mostly hit or miss, with very little if any real enthusiasm. The drafting starts in the afternoon, then goes on into the evening. On rare occasions, it may have an extra session the afternoon after.

The first-round draft choice comes quickly. Each professional football club has scouted its prospects well and grabs off its first pick with no fuss or bother if it's lucky. If not, it has a second and third choice handy.

The drafting for the 1956 football season began in its usual speedy manner. The first-round draft choices were made quickly. Bart Starr of Alabama was not among them. No one expected him to be. As a matter of fact, there were few coaches at the meeting who had even heard of the young quarterback.

The second-round choices were made, and then the third round. No one called out, "Bart Starr."

One hundred, a hundred and fifty college players had been selected for tryouts with the big National League football clubs. Still no team selected Bart Starr.

The coaches had gone through their sixteenth round of drafting, when Bart's name was finally mentioned; not as a choice, but as a possibility.

"Johnny Dee mentioned a kid by the name of Bart Starr."

"Where does he play?"

"Quarterback."

The contingent of coaches and scouts from Green Bay were talking.

"What do you know about him?"

"Only what Johnny Dee wrote in his letter."

"What's that?"

"He says the kid can pass."

"Yeah?"

"He says he's pretty smart, Phi Beta Kappa or something."

"If he's that smart, he might be the kind of quarterback we can develop."

There wasn't any eagerness about the selection, but Green Bay was in a position where any kind of help was desperately needed. The Packers drafted Bart Starr in the seventeenth round. As far as the football world was concerned at that time and place, Bart Starr was hardly a major prospect for the professional game, and certainly not a very good one at that. A seventeenth-round draft choice isn't likely to be more than a run-of-the-mill ballplayer, someone who isn't going to make a starting lineup, and certainly someone who isn't going to make the headlines on the sports pages.

Nevertheless, when Bart got the news, back home in Montgomery, he was elated, as only a young fellow with dreams of glory on the gridiron can be elated by a request to try out for a major football team.

"I know it's Green Bay," he said. "But it's big league football."

He didn't dance a jig. He didn't go running into the streets with his good news. That wasn't the kind of fellow Bart Starr was, or is. He was happy enough, but he was not without doubts.

"I haven't played much. Not this year," he said.

"You'll make it," said his good friends.

"I'm going to give it my very best," said Bart.

"Green Bay?" said Cherry. "Where is this place?"

His life-long pal, Bobby Barnes, said, "Bart was worried. He was worried that the almost two years of idleness had robbed him of his passing skill, of his confidence, of his ability to marshall a team and to move that team up the field.

"He wasn't really pessimistic about his chances. Bart has always been an optimistic individual. He always thinks and feels that everything is going to turn out all right.

"But he hadn't done much in football for a couple of years. There was that trouble with his back which kept him out of the game most of his junior year at Alabama. Then there was this last year, with the coach keeping him on the bench for most of the season. He just wasn't quite sure of himself. He had doubts."

Bart had doubts, all right, but he had the will, the desire and the drive to make up for them.

He had received one other offer to play professional ball, from the Hamilton Tigers of the Canadian Football League. They were offering him $6,500 for a season of play in Canada.

"What do you think?" he asked Cherry.

Cherry was now Mrs. Bart Starr.

Bart had borrowed a car from his pal, Bobby Barnes, one night, while they were still both at school.

"We're going to get married," he had announced.

It wasn't a long trip over the Alabama state line, and Cherry and Bart became Mr. and Mrs.

It was just like Bart and Cherry to elope, to have a very quiet and very private wedding. They were very private people. Even their families were kept in the dark about their intentions, and consented to the marriage only after the fact.

If Cherry had an opinion on which club Bart should choose—Green Bay or the Canadian—she didn't say. She knew as well as Bart the club he would select. It was Bart's pride as well as his need to prove to himself that would make the decision.

"Green Bay," he said. "They're offering me a chance to make it in the National Football League, and I've got to take it."

The night before he left for Green Bay, Bart and Cherry and Bobby and his wife, Norma, sat down to a quiet dinner.

"Tomorrow is the big day," said Bobby.

"Yeah," said Bart.

"We're going to miss you, but we're glad to see you go," said Bobby.

"We'll miss you, too," said Bart.

That is the kind of evening it was. A very quiet evening, just the way Bart and Cherry would have it.

There was nothing in the local press, no big newspaper story, nothing on the radio or television, no big send-off. It might as well have been any other ordinary evening in Montgomery, Alabama.

It wasn't, of course.

"I guess we were all a little apprehensive," says Bobby Barnes. "Not exactly worried, but apprehensive."

Apprehension or no, however, it was a significant evening for Bart Starr, the eve of his leaving to join the Green Bay Packers, the eve of one of the greatest careers in football history.

CHAPTER 8

On the evening of August 11, 1919, a group of husky young men got together for a meeting in the offices of the Green Bay *Press-Gazette*. Seated on desks, on the floor, on chairs, the group listened with growing interest to "Curly" Lambeau on the possibilities of forming a semiprofessional football team in Green Bay.

Curly, whose dad, Marcel Lambeau, was one of the leading building contractor's in Green Bay, had been a local football and track star at East High School and upon graduation had traveled to South Bend, Indiana, to enroll in school and to play football for Notre Dame. Curly had starred with the 1918 Notre Dame team, coached by the immortal Knute Rockne. At Notre Dame Curly's teammates had included such Notre Dame stars as the great George Gipp, Eddie Anderson, Hunk Anderson, Clipper Smith, Norm Barry, Charley Crowley, and the Irish playing an abbreviated schedule in 1918 had lost but 1 game to Michigan State.

The football season over, Curly returned home to Green Bay where he was hired as the foreman of the receiving department at the Acme Packing Company for a handsome salary of $250 per month. But as the waning months of summer blended into autumn, Lambeau began to think and plan for some kind of football, as he had made up his mind to continue working and would not return to Notre Dame. It was for that purpose that he had gathered together a group of former East High School and West High School players to talk with them about organizing a Green Bay eleven.

"It's a great idea to start a team," one of the men said. "But what do we do about uniforms?" "Where do we get some money?" "Where do we practice?" "Who will coach the team?"

Curly Lambeau spoke up, "I've already got some of the answers to those questions," he said. "I talked to Mr. Frank Peck. You fellows all know him. He's one of our top officers at the Acme Packing Company. Mr. Peck has already said he'll give me $500, which is just what we need for the uniforms. Now, as to coaching the team. I think I know enough, at least I know and learned a great deal from Coach Rockne at Notre Dame. I can coach the team, and I've got Bill Ryan, West High's Coach. He will be my chief assistant."

And so the Green Bay Packers were born. In 1919, the first year of football, the Packers won 10 games in a row, and had the town rooters solidly behind them. In 1921 the Packers joined president Jim Thorpe of the National Football League in forming a new league, which included such teams as Chicago, Cleveland, Detroit, Akron, Canton, Rock Island, Rochester, Buffalo, Dayton, and Columbus.

Like most of the professional football teams in those

days, the Packers lost money regularly and soon the Acme Packing Company, which had been paying some of the outstanding bills, said it could no longer afford to make up those losses. And so Andy Turnbull, a top newspaper man with the Green Bay *Press-Gazette* invited a number of Green Bay's business men to join him at lunch at the Beaumont Hotel. The men who joined Mr. Turnbull—Lee Joannes, Dr. Kelly, Gerry Clifford, Emmet Platten, and E. C. Witteberg—pitched in with some $2,500 to pay off some of the Packer debts, and several weeks later offered Packer stock to the citizens of Green Bay.

Today, several thousands of Green Bay citizens—salesmen, druggists, clerks—own shares in the Green Bay Packers. Some own $1,000, $1,500, or $5,000 worth. And when the team wins they are delighted. When the Packers lose, each owner is sure he knows what went wrong and offers the coach his advice.

The Green Bay Packers had developed into the most feared, the most powerful team in professional football. In 1929, 1930, and 1931 they had been world champions. Three years in a row they were almost unbeatable. Head coach Curly Lambeau had such great stars like Carl Hubbard, Clarke Hinkle, Arnie Herber, Bo Molenda, and Johnny Blood on their roster, and they rolled over every other team in the league to finish the 1929 season undefeated. In 1930, against a much improved opposition, they won 10 and lost only 3, to top the League again. They repeated in 1931, winning 12 and losing just 2.

They couldn't make it four championships in a row,

but they were never far from the top of the League in the four years that followed. In 1936, however, they resumed their leadership in the football world with a 10-1-1 record.

In 1938, with the addition of such luminaries as Don Hutson and Cecil Isbell, Coach Curly Lambeau led the Packers to the Western Division championship of the League with an 8–3 record. In 1939, with 9 wins against 2 defeats, they were champions of the football world once more.

A 10 and 1 record in 1941 wasn't good enough, and the Packers lost the football crown to the amazing Chicago Bears. But, with a squad that included Ben Starret, Irv Comp, Larry Craig, Dick Bilda, Tony Canadeo, Paul Duhart, Bob Kahler, Ted Fritsch, Don Perkins, Roy McKay, Joe Laws, and the immortal record-breaking end, Don Hutson—all men whose feats on the gridiron will not be forgotten—the Green Bay Packers took the world football championship once more.

That was in 1944.

From that year on, and for the next fifteen years, it was all pretty much downhill for the Packers. For a while, Green Bay was able to eke out just enough wins to keep a shade over the 500 per cent mark. In 1948, however, they went into a nose dive, dropping 9 of the 12 games of the season. In 1949 they could win but 2 of the games in what must have seemed to them to be an endless football year. They were to experience seasons that were even worse.

Despite their poor overall record, the Packers were still a major league football team, a name to be reckoned with. They were a team that competed against the greatest names in professional football, and in 1956 Bart Starr was determined to make that team. He was reasonably confident that he could make the squad, if he could recapture the skills and confidence that made him one of the most talked about sophomore quarterbacks in Alabama history. To that end, he decided on a program of activities that would bring him into the Packer camp in August in the very finest physical and mental condition. It was a program that demanded the utmost effort and concentration in his young life, and it demanded all of his waking hours throughout the spring and summer months; it even included effort on the part of his wife, Cherry.

The smoldering summer sun hung down like a huge fiery ball, hot and unbearable over the back yard of a pleasant, comfortable residence in Jackson, Mississippi, as a tall, broad-shouldered lithe young man in T shirt and shorts sharply called out signals. Suddenly, a football was shoveled to him by an attractive, slender girl.

The young man sprinted some ten yards to his left, pivoted sharply and with an easy, fluid motion threw the football at a target some twenty yards away. There, hanging on a rope, tied to the limb of a tree, dangled an automobile tire. The ball whistled through the tire, hitting the ground and bouncing up and away. The girl wearily chased after the ball, scooped it up and again tossed the ball back to the young man.

"That's great, Cherry," said Bart. "I'm feeling pretty good now. Getting that rhythm and freedom in my arm. Now I'm going to try a couple of jump passes."

He paced off about twenty steps, leaped into the air, aimed the ball, cocked his arm and fired the ball cleanly through the tire. Cherry once more picked up the ball and threw it back to Bart.

Cherry and Bart had been doing this all afternoon on this torrid summer's day. All summer long, in fact, Bart had been throwing footballs at this tire, sharpening his passing eye, his timing, so he would be ready when he reported to the Green Bay Packers.

Bart knew he had some catching up to do. He was going to camp to battle four or five quarterbacks, who had had either college or professional experience, and who had played some ten or twelve games the season before. Starr had played very little the past two years. He was rusty and he needed every advantage.

Bart studied the roster of the Green Bay Packers. He read every news story, every item that pertained to Green Bay. He called on coaches, friends of his, to fill him in on the Packers' offense. He studied the game reports and statistics for the 1955 season; a season in which the Packers had won 6 games while losing 6. He particularly read with interest, everything he could find in the sports magazines about Tobin Rote, the outstanding Packer quarterback, who came out of Rice University in 1949, joined Green Bay in 1950 and directed the Packers for six uneventful years.

Just as important, Bart kept close watch on his diet. He kept good hours. He was up early in the morning running through the back streets and alleys of Jackson, to keep his all-around physical condition up to par. And when he went to bed at night he kept the Holy Bible on a table near his bed. Bart Starr would always have the Holy Bible near his bed wherever he traveled, wherever he slept. He didn't talk much about his religion, but Bart was a religious man, and his faith, undoubtedly, as it has been for others, and will be for others, was a source of great personal strength.

Bart had done everything he could to get himself ready for Green Bay, and by early August, he was in top physical and mental condition for the almost impossible job of breaking into the line-up of the Packers. He was ready for anything Lisle Blackbourn, the Packers' head coach, would demand of him. He was ready, too, for the host of Green Bay Packer fans who were sure to examine and evaluate every single move he made on the field.

CHAPTER 9

Green Bay is a small town. Its population is just about 60,000. It doesn't seem reasonable to expect a town of 60,000 to support a big league professional football team, but it does. The football fans in Detroit, Pittsburgh, Dallas, Chicago, New York, or in any of the other big cities with a football franchise, may be rabid. There is nothing in the world, however, that compares with the fervor, with the loyalty, with the sheer madness of the fans in Green Bay, Wisconsin.

They eat football, they drink football, they sleep football, and they dream football. The day the Packers win, the town goes wild with celebration. Every Packer win is the occasion for a national holiday in Green Bay. When the Packers lose, it is an occasion in Green Bay for crepe.

Bart Starr had heard about these rabid Green Bay Packer fans. He had mixed feelings about it. Such rabid support must put an extra burden on a ballplayer, must ask him to perform at levels that are at times unreachable. On the other hand, it is this kind of loyalty—so consistent with the Packer fans—this kind of encouragement that has to greatly inspire a ballplayer.

"Go, team! Go!"

"How often have I heard that roar?" thought Starr. "And how often has it turned on the adrenalin and made me play just that much harder?"

Trepidation and hope, both came into Green Bay, Wisconsin, with Bart Starr. Yet, for whatever fears still chipped away at his thinking, his feeling, Bart was quite confident he was going to make the squad, become a member of the Green Bay Packers.

Lisle Blackbourn was the Packers' head coach in 1956. Blackbourn had been a star at little Lawrence College and upon graduation, coached at Washington High School in Milwaukee. Lisle compiled a tremendous record in the twenty-two years at Washington High—his teams won 140 games, while losing but 6. He then came to Wisconsin where he assisted Harry Stuhldreher as an assistant coach, then took over as line coach, then head coach at Marquette University.

Blackbourn was the popular choice to succeed Packers' Coach, Gene Ronzini in 1954, after the Packer officials decided something had to be done, something drastic to give the Packers a new look after six dismal, losing seasons.

Blackbourn's record during the first two years of his reign was a mite better than Ronzini's. The 1954 Packers won 4 games, while they lost 8. In 1955 Blackbourn had the Packers winning 6 games, while losing 6. It was their best record in eight years.

Blackbourn got several fine players in the 1956 draft,

and traded for such fine players as Gary Knafelc, Howie Ferguson, and Bill Howton. The starting quarterback was the veteran Tobin Rote. Rote was a seven-year veteran who knew that his team was saddled with players who were merely playing out their contracts, going nowhere. They were losers on a losing ball club. But Tobin was the kind of man who seemed to be bothered by nothing. Basically he was a fine quarterback, who knew every angle of his job and knew it well. It was fortunate for Bart Starr that he roomed with Rote. Rote liked him and wanted to help him with his game and, as a matter of fact, went out of his way to do so.

"He taught me a lot," Bart Starr says of Rote.

"Zip that ball," said Rote. "You won't make this team if you loft the ball to your receivers. Don't throw those soft, cream puffs. Particularly, when you throw those short passes, you have to really zing 'em. That way you won't be intercepted."

"I admired his courage, too," says Bart.

Bart watched Rote go down and roll away under a vicious tackle, then get back to his feet as though nothing at all had touched him.

"You've got to be able to hold onto the ball when you've got no receiver open," said Rote. "Don't throw the ball in a desperation attempt if you don't spot your receiver.

"It's give and take," said Tobin Rote. "Try to relax and roll with the tackle when those big linemen hit you. Don't try to fight them off. You're a quarterback. Not a fullback. You won't get hurt if you learn how to fall."

Bart adjusted his thinking, began to throw the ball with greater speed and on a line to his receivers. He studied the pass patterns of his receivers and practiced hour after hour, day after day. He began to study the films of the opposing teams to learn their defensive moves, and ever so slowly his confidence came back to him.

As the training season began to draw to a close, the Packer roster had to be pared. Those were the days and the nights that Bart began to dread.

Every day, then, there was a knock on some player's door and one of the assistant coaches would be saying, to one of the rookies, "So sorry."

The routine went something like this:

"You know that we have to cut the squad. We can't carry that many players. It's a League rule. Now, you've got a lot of good stuff, but I'm afraid we can't use you this year. Maybe you can sign on with some other team. Good Luck!"

"The Turk" was what the players called the assistant coach who delivered the sad words, "I'm sorry."

The players who had, to the moment, escaped the squad cut never mentioned the assistant coach by name. It was bad luck, they were sure, to call him by his name. He was simply "The Turk."

"The Turk has struck again."

Nor did they ever speak of the rookie—or sometimes a veteran—who had been cut by the squad. That was considered bad luck, too.

Every rookie who ever tried to make a big league club has had the same experience. He knows the step of "The

Turk," the measure of its stride, the weight of the foot-
fall. He listens to it as it sounds through the halls of the
camp at night, and his heart stops—or seems to stop
anyway—as it approaches his door. If "The Turk" stops
at his door, he knows the speech he is going to hear
and, of course, he is never fully prepared for it. If the
step continues past his door, the rookie executes a deep
sigh of relief and his heart starts to beat normally again.

Bart Starr was no exception to the rule. He was as
vulnerable as the rest to the fears that struck with the
first steps of "The Turk" in his hallway.

"I was never sure I had made the club," says Bart,
"not that first year, until the final cuts were announced.
It was quite an experience."

And when he finally learned that he had survived the
cuts, that he had made the team, "It was one of the
happiest days in my life," says Bart.

Lisle Blackbourn did not play Bart very much that
first season. He would send Bart into a game when it
was all but over and lost, perhaps, just to give him a bit
of action and encouragement.

"I wasn't very good," Bart said. "But I wasn't too
bad."

As always, Bart underrated his performance. Losing
cause or not, he did his best, and Blackbourn must have
been impressed with what he saw, for he kept him on
the team. In his first year Bart threw 44 passes and completed 24, for a 54 per cent average. There were few, if
any rookie quarterbacks in the NFL who did as well, but
Bart was not very happy with his freshman year at

Green Bay for the team managed to win but 4 games, while losing 8.

Summing up that first season Bart said, "We didn't win many games and I didn't play much, but I sure learned an awful lot."

Bart Starr was a keen student of football. He was a listener and he asked questions. He knew every play in the Packers' play book, and he knew a great deal about his opponents' strategy. He studied their offense and defense; he was in the film library, night and day, and he began to notice certain plays, certain strategies that he would be able to use later on.

Coach Lisle Blackbourn was impressed with Starr. He wasn't too sure that Bart could throw well enough to be his Number One quarterback, but he knew that Bart had a keen football mind. He didn't think Starr had a good arm. Bart had to prove it.

CHAPTER 10

The Packers signed Paul Hornung in 1957. Tagged "The Golden Boy" at Notre Dame where he electrified the nation with his marvelous running and passing as the All-American quarterback of the "Fighting Irish," Paul was one of those God-given athletes who had everything his own way. At Flaget High School in Louisville, Paul was a standout basketball and football star during his four years and was voted the greatest high school football star in Kentucky. In 1956 Hornung won the coveted Heisman Trophy, awarded annually to the nation's top college football star. His spectacular all-around play at Notre Dame had all the big-time professional scouts standing at his doorstep, fighting to sign him to a pro contract.

Bart Starr recognized that with Paul Hornung and Tobin Rote on the Packer roster his chances for becoming the Number One quarterback for Green Bay, or even the back-up man for Number One, were highly diminished. Still, Bart wasn't a man to give up in any kind of battle. If nothing else, he was more determined to fight it out with Hornung, Rote, or anyone else for that position. He would not allow his dream to die.

He worked at keeping himself in shape all winter, spring, and summer. He kept practicing his passing, concentrating on speed and accuracy at the practice target. He was determined to give his best to the game; he told himself that he had to have the patience to wait for the right time and the right place, when the call would come for him to lead his team into the gridiron battles; he was determined to prove to coach Blackbourn that he could be and would be Number One, and when he reported for practice that summer, Bart was ready for the challenge.

As the preseason practice sessions progressed, Starr, Rote, and Hornung battled for the Number One quarterback position. Rote had the experience, but Starr, improving each day, became a real threat, while Hornung showed flashes of the marvelous all-around ability he had displayed at Notre Dame. Paul could run, kick and block, but when he threw the football, he was intercepted time after time. Paul threw one "cream puff" pass after another. (Tobin Rote called Hornung's passes, "cream puffs" because they were soft and easy to intercept.)

Blackbourn fretted. He had hoped that Hornung would answer his great need for a first-rate quarterback; a man who could run, direct the team, and really throw the ball. Tobin Rote was a good man, but his best years as a quarterback were behind him. And his backup quarterbacks were something less than he wanted, than he needed. Blackbourn had great respect and a genuine lik-

6. Bart and his father—Sergeant Ben Starr.

7. Starr played in the annual college All-Star game.

8. Bart and his Frank Thomas Memorial Trophy after his graduation from Alabama. He also won the Jimmy Moore Memorial Trophy for being the Alabama athlete with the highest scholarship average for that year. He made straight A's in his final two semesters.

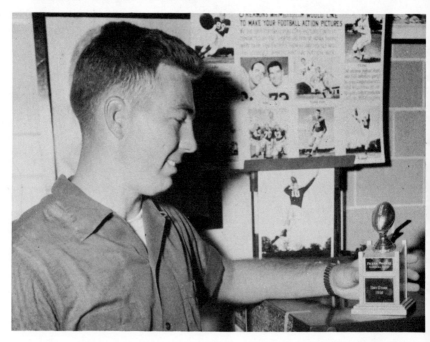

9. Coach Lombardi giving Bart a bit of advice. Things didn't always go too well on the field. (*Vernon J. Biever Photo*)

10. Starr, the young Green Bay quarterback, about to hand off.

ing for Bart Starr, but Starr had no real pro experience and his ability to pass in the pro league was questionable.

Meanwhile, Blackbourn had to do something drastic to strengthen his team at that vital quarterback position. He swung a big trade with the Detroit Lions for Tobin Rote and in return got Vito "Babe" Parilli, the former Kentucky All-American.

When he was at Lanier High School in Montgomery, Bart had all but worshipped Parilli. The Babe was his favorite pinup star, and he had photographs of Parilli pasted all over the walls of his bedroom. He had met Parilli at Kentucky and the Babe had been very nice to Bart. Bart never forgot his kindness. Now, he was suddenly face to face with him, battling to take his job as Number One quarterback for the Green Bay Packers.

He wasn't about to take that job away from Parilli, however; not yet, not with the way Blackbourn saw the situation and estimated the capabilities of Starr. Still, Bart gave it all he had, and coach Blackbourn saw fit to give the young quarterback considerably more playing time than he had had in 1956.

Parilli, a gentle sort of man, wasn't shaken by the competition Bart gave him. On the contrary, he looked on the younger quarterback as a kind of kid brother, and he treated him that way.

"You want to cup your hands this way," said Babe Parilli, demonstrating the gesture for the younger player. "That way you get a better handle on the ball on the snap from center."

"You get back into the pocket fast," said the Babe.

"Run! Then release the ball fast, once you spot your intended receiver. You can't waste a second. You can't waste half a second. Remember, the defense isn't out there just to watch you toss the ball. They're there to get you before you have a chance to throw it."

Bart Starr learned. He learned fast. He had always been and he would always be an excellent student—in class and on the gridiron.

Bart had watched Babe Parilli play at Kentucky.

"I learned from him then," he says, "while I was still a schoolboy. I remembered what I had learned from Parilli, and it had helped me no little when I played ball in Alabama.

"There is no end to what Parilli taught me, when he came to Green Bay," he says. "As a matter of fact, he taught me more about the basic techniques in playing quarterback than any coach up to that year."

Bart threw 215 passes in that 1957 football season with Green Bay, as he started most of the games that season. He had 117 completions for 1,489 yards, 3 touchdowns and a passing average of 54.4 per cent. It was a better than an average season for a backup quarterback, but neither Starr nor Parilli could lift the Packers out of their doldrums. In 1957 Green Bay could win only 3 of its games and lose 9.

When a club has several losing seasons in a row, someone has to pay for it. Most often, it is the coach. It doesn't matter that the front office has neglected to obtain the players needed to bolster the club's offense or defense. It doesn't matter that it is obvious to everybody —front office, players, fans—that the club just hasn't the

power to score consistently, to defend its goal line consistently. The head coach is held responsible for the dismal showing of the club, and he's got to go. This is true
in college sports as well as in professional. In baseball,
basketball, track, football, whatever, after a losing season,
the coach goes.

Lisle Blackbourn didn't wait to be fired. He resigned
and went back to his old job at Marquette University.

It was at this point that Blackbourn let it all out for
Bart Starr.

"You're not going to find it easy making it in the
pros," he said to Bart. "The fact is, I don't think you'll
ever make more than backup quarterback. Is that what
you want?"

"No, sir," said Bart. "That's not what I want."

"Of course it's not what you want," said Blackbourn.
"You play backup for a couple of years, and then you're
out."

"That's not my way of looking at it, sir," responded
Bart. "I expect to stick it out. I want to be the Number
One quarterback, and that's what I'll be, sir."

Blackbourn backed off a bit.

"You understand the game all right," said the resigning coach. "You've learned a lot these last couple of
years. You learn fast. You've got a fine head on your
shoulders, but I don't know about being Number One. I
think you could be a great help teaching. You're a natural."

"School?" queried Bart.

"I mean coaching," came back Blackbourn. "I think
you'd be a great help, coaching quarterbacks."

"That's not what I want to do, sir," said Bart. "I've never thought of myself as a coach. I want to play, sir."

Blackbourn then finally came out with what he had had in mind all along.

"How about coming with me to Marquette University?"

Bart was too stunned to answer.

"As an assistant coach," said Blackbourn.

For anyone else, with Bart's limited experience in both college and professional football, this would have been a marvelous offer he couldn't refuse. For anyone else, who had been told by a professional football coach that he would never make the starting line-up of a professional football club, this alternative would have been something like a gift out of the heavens. Not for Bart Starr.

"Thank you, sir," he said. "It's very good of you, sir," he said. "But I can't go with you to Marquette."

"Why not?" demanded Blackbourn. "You're not going to get anywhere here with Green Bay. Marquette will open the door for you. You could become a fine coach."

"Thank you, sir," said Bart again. "I'm not moving. Not just yet. I'm going to stay in Green Bay as long as I can, as long as they'll have me. I've got to try to make it as a pro quarterback before I try anything else."

Dedication, perseverance, determination, and perhaps a bit of pride, were the basic characteristics in the make-up of Bart Starr. He had set himself a goal and he was going to attain it.

He would reach it, for all the lack of confidence he

was yet to encounter in the coaches who came to guide the football destiny of the Green Bay Packers. He would reach it, despite all the adverse opinion that came his way from people who should perhaps have known better. He would attain that goal for all the hours he had to sit it out on the bench, for all the years his magnificent abilities on the gridiron were underestimated by both coaches and fans, and sportswriters as well, for all the seasons he was just passed by. He would make it, reach that goal he had set for himself, attain it; but it was going to take time, and time has a way of running out on a professional football player.

CHAPTER 11

"It was like musical chairs," says Bart Starr.

He was talking about the season of 1958, and how he and Babe Parilli were shuffled in and out of the Green Bay Packer quarterback spot.

"Babe was in there most of the time," says Bart, "and when Joe Francis wasn't calling the signals, McLean would send me in to do the job."

Joe Francis was Number One backup quarterback for the Packers, or Number Two backup man, depending on how Coach McLean felt about Bart Starr for any particular game.

McLean was Ray "Scooter" McLean, the man Green Bay had hired to replace Lisle Blackbourn as head coach of the Packers. The front office figured that McLean, an assistant under Blackbourn, could improve on the 1957 record of the Green Bay squad, 3 victories and 9 losses. They were wrong. The Packers, under McLean, took a precipitous nose dive to the bottom of the League. All the pleading, cajoling and hard work of the coach, the front office, and the fans was to no avail as the Packers managed to win but one game all year long. It was the poorest year in Green Bay football history.

Babe Parilli just couldn't move the team.

"When I got into the game," says Bart, "I just didn't do the job."

Jerry Kramer came out of the University of Idaho to join the Packers in 1958. He was to become one of professional football's all-time greats. Five times he was to be named All-National Football League linesman. Always an astute observer of the game and its players, he was to become one of the best commentators on the sport. Yet, writing of that first season of his with the Green Bay Packers, he said, "I swear I have absolutely no recollection of Bart Starr playing that year. None at all. He threw more than 150 passes that season, so I must have seen him. I must have seen him a lot. But he made no impression on me. Most of that year was a total loss. Nobody played well."

That was the kind of football year it was for Bart and the Packers.

"I lost confidence," he says. "I wasn't sure about the plays I called. I lost confidence in my passing."

Confidence, more than perhaps everything else, is basic to a successful career in any competitive sport.

With the kind of offense Green Bay had, Bart Starr suffered more interceptions than he had ever experienced before, in school, in college, or with the Packers.

"Every time I was intercepted, it would kill me," he says. "It would have me worried the rest of the game. You can't play a good game when you're worried that way. In 1958, I was worried all the time."

This failure on the field did more than worry him. He became irritable, irascible. He couldn't take criticism. A nasty word, or what seemed to him to be a nasty word, from the coach on the side lines, about one play or another he had called, and Bart Starr would jump.

This was indeed strange behavior for a young man who was known to be the politest of ballplayers. No matter how badly a play had been bungled, he'd keep his mouth shut, never chew out the offender.

" 'Let's go, Jerry,' Bart shouted in the huddle. But after the game, he came up to me in the locker room and apologized," said Kramer.

"I'm sorry. I didn't mean to holler at you," said Bart.

Only the kind of frustrating year Bart had in that season of 1958 could account for his almost belligerent reaction to even the slightest criticism of his performance on the gridiron.

Bart tends to laugh it off a bit when he is reminded of this uncharacteristic behavior on his part. "I was sensitive about criticism that year," he admits. Then, with half a wink, he adds, "I'm a sensitive man, basically. Ask my wife, Cherry."

If that remark doesn't get the laugh from his listeners, he'll add, for the sure response, "At least, that's what she says. She's always telling me how sensitive I am. And I've got to believe my wife, don't I?"

It wasn't funny, however, for Bart in 1958.

It had been a terrible year, and the young quarterback took off for home, after that last miserable game of the season, feeling as deflated about his future as any aspiring young football player could possibly feel about his future.

"I was discouraged," says Starr. "I knew perhaps better than anyone else how poorly I had performed for the Packers."

He needed more game experience, calling the plays, leading his team down the field, a lot more experience than his coaches had allowed him. In a sense, his three years with the Green Bay Packers had been a continuation of his experience in the last year of play at the University of Alabama, when he was sent in to direct the Crimson Tide attack with such infrequency and only after the game had been lost.

"I wasn't mature enough," he says, evaluating those three years with the Packers. "I wasn't emotionally mature enough to give Green Bay the kind of leadership a quarterback is expected to give his club."

If Bart thought of quitting the game, he didn't say. It is doubtful, though, that if the thought of getting out of football did occasionally occur to him, it ever stayed with him for very long. The old dedication, the old desire to achieve, would soon dispell even his most pessimistic thoughts.

"Bart is essentially an optimist," his closest friends knew, and often said.

Still, Bart would refer to the letdown he had suffered in his senior year at Alabama.

"Just sitting there on the bench, doing nothing," said Bart of his last year with the Crimson Tide, "cut into my confidence."

Without any confidence a man is no good to his team

or himself. How do you develop confidence, or regain the confidence you once had?

Bart Starr had the answer to that question.

"The only way to build confidence," he said, "is to succeed. Success comes first. Then confidence follows. For three or four years," he added, "I haven't succeeded at anything in football; the last year at Alabama and the three I've been with the Packers."

The opportunity for Bart Starr was coming, along with the opportunity to regain the confidence he once had; but he would have to wait for both, and for what must have been for him a very long time.

Meanwhile, Bart had a lot of thinking to do. So did the front office in Green Bay, Wisconsin.

It was obvious to everyone that Scooter McLean was finished with the Packers. His one season as the Green Bay head coach had been the Packers' worst season ever. McLean was one of the nicest of men in the gridiron game. But he couldn't pull the team, however little talent it had, together.

There were cliques among the players, and cliques don't make for teamplay and teamwork; and McLean did nothing about breaking them up and unifying the club. He did nothing about getting his men into good physical condition, and good physical condition is a prerequisite for any professional athlete. Nor did he object any too strenuously as the players went through their practice sessions in a dispirited, half-hearted effort. Nor did he say much when a man loafed on a play, failed to block, casually dropped a forward pass, made none of the great individual effort expected of a player in a game.

Some of the players broke every curfew law. McLean knew that they were all taking advantage of his good nature, but it was his good nature that wouldn't allow him to do anything about it.

It was baseball's Leo Durocher who said, "Nice guys come in last."

Scooter McLean's squad came in last.

What Durocher didn't say was that nice guys don't last in professional football. With perhaps the single exception of Bart Starr, this is pretty much a fact.

In any case, Scooter McLean didn't last long with the Green Bay Packers. With the end of the 1958 season Scooter was through. The problem that faced the front office in Green Bay was: Where can we find someone to replace him? Where can we find somebody who can pull this team together? Where can we find a coach who can turn this club into the winner it once was? Where do we find a good teacher, disciplinarian, leader?

Maybe it was fate. Maybe it was just sheer luck. But for once, the front office in Green Bay, Wisconsin, chose the right man for the right job. They couldn't have done any better.

The man they asked to take on the post of head coach of the Green Bay Packers was Vince Lombardi.

"Who is Vince Lombardi?" asked Jerry Kramer, when Jerry got the news in some corner of a sports page.

"He's with the New York Giants," was the answer he got. "Assistant coach."

"That's dumb!" exploded Jerry. "How can they hire someone who's never been a head coach? How can they hire somebody who hasn't proved what he can do? How stupid can they get?"

Kramer was to discover very quickly that for once the Green Bay front office hadn't been "stupid," that for once they had pulled off a very smart deal.

Jerry had reported in at the training camp a few days early, and was taking things easy. He started to leave the camp dormitory with his golf clubs when he was stopped.

"Where are you going?" asked Lombardi.

"To play golf," said Kramer.

"When you're in the dormitory," said Lombardi, quietly but firmly, "you make all your meals, all practices, all meetings, and all curfews and no golf, just like everybody else."

It was obvious that Vince Lombardi was no Scooter McLean.

CHAPTER 12

Vince Lombardi was a football legend while he was still alive. He is still a legend in the world of professional football. When he played football for the Fordham Rams back in the 1930s, Vince was one of the immovable, "Seven Blocks of Granite." It was the Ram line that threw back enemy ball carriers as though they had banged into a cement wall, and the Fordham team of that era was ranked as one of the nation's great elevens. Upon graduating with high honors, Vince played pro football with the Wilmington Clippers, studied law at Fordham, sold insurance, and helped out with the family finances by working in the research laboratory of the Dupont Company in Wilmington, Delaware.

In 1939 Vince gave it all up to take a job as an assistant coach of football at St. Cecelia High School in Teaneck, New Jersey; he moved up to the head coaching job in 1942, and then proceeded to turn out teams that won thirty-six consecutive victories in a row, during a six-year period. He then moved up the ladder to Fordham University, where he took over as coach of the

Fordham Freshman team. Under Coach Lombardi, the Ram freshmen were undefeated.

In 1948 Coach Earl "Red" Blaik appointed Vince his assistant coach at West Point, and Lombardi patiently molded the Army's offensive teams in the next five years, to where they compiled one of the most consistently high-scoring records in the nation.

In 1953 Vince was appointed offensive coach of the New York Giants of the National League, and by 1956 had the Giants battling the Baltimore Colts for the world championship.

Lombardi could be just as tough with the owners of a club as he could be with the players. "This is the way I'm going to run the club. This is what I want," he snapped when he came to Green Bay. President Domenic Olejiniczak, president of the Packers, and anxious to get the team winning again, made Lombardi the general manager—thus giving him the power to make any trade, fire any player.

Lombardi walked into his Packer office one cold day in January, looked around the empty offices, picked up a raft of yellow legal pads, and went upstairs to a little darkened office where he would sit and watch every film of the 1958 Packer games and make notes on them.

It was late the next day, in the middle of a film of a game with the Chicago Bears, when Vince rose out of his chair and told one of his coaches to stop the film and run that play over again.

Up on the screen, Paul Hornung was running out of left halfback against the Bears. It was a simple play. Hornung started out wide, then made that big swinging cutback of his and crashed into tackle and dragged a couple of big Chicago linemen with him as he went for 14 yards.

"Run that play, again," Lombardi said.

The coach ran it again.

"You're looking at my offense," Lombardi said. He collared Hornung the next day. "You're my left halfback from now on," he told Paul.

"In New York we built our offense around Frank Gifford. He played left half. Now we're in Green Bay. You're going to be the guy we build an offense around. You can do it. Do you have any questions?"

Hornung had none. For the first time in his pro-football career he was getting a clear shot at making it big. From this point on Hornung began to rip the opposition to shreds.

"When I first studied the Packer films," said Vince, "I decided that Hornung was going to be our left halfback, and the next thing I needed was lots of quarterback help. So I traded for Lamar McHan."

"The first thing I needed was help at quarterback." A glum Bart Starr read what Lombardi had said. His confidence was now down to near zero. "I don't blame coach Lombardi for trading for McHan," Bart told Bobby Barnes. "We do need help. I haven't been doing the job. And now it looks like I'll be waiting, sitting on the bench another year."

There would be waiting. There would be trial and error. There would be plenty of frustration. But it would be coach Vince Lombardi who would discover and develop the great potential in young Bart Starr.

Lombardi didn't release Bart, but he didn't give him any reason to celebrate either. Lamar McHan was the odds-on favorite to be the Number One quarterback, Joe Francis was designated the backup man. Bart Starr was relegated to the third spot on the Packer quarterback roster.

Another less-determined player might have given up, packed up his gear, and gone home to look for another career—any career but football. But Bart Starr felt he had to work harder, study harder, know more than the other man.

"For all the disappointments, for all my failures," Bart said, "there was still nothing I wanted more than to play football. I don't know whether it was just determination or pride that kept me going. Maybe it was both."

What Bart didn't know, and what might have given him considerably more courage and hope, was that Vince Lombardi's opinion of him, and of his playing, was not entirely negative. On the contrary, though Lombardi never told him so, certainly not in that first year, the coach was impressed by his young player.

Years later Vince Lombardi was to write of Bart, "He impressed me right from the beginning with the way he went about getting himself ready for the game. I was impressed by his memory. I was impressed by his dedication. I was impressed by his desire."

Confidence. That was the all-important quality Bart Starr needed, as Vince saw it and as Bart knew well enough. But it is success that brings about confidence, and Bart had had little opportunity to prove himself successful as the 1959 football season opened.

Lombardi used the free hand given him by the front office in a remarkable manner. In addition to McHan, he got Fred Thurston from Baltimore; Henry Jordan, Lew Carpenter, Bobby Freeman and Bill Quinlan from Cleveland, to bolster the Packer attack. To strengthen the Green Bay defensive unit, he picked up safety man Emlen Tunnel from the New York Giants, and guard, John Dittrich. He also signed Boyd Dowler, who in his first year at Green Bay was to be voted the Rookie of the Year in the National League.

Lombardi drove himself hard. He drove his men hard.

"You'd better take off some weight," he said to linebacker Tom Bettis.

"I'm built that way," protested the linebacker.

"Get it off!" snapped Lombardi, "or pack up your equipment!"

He was quick to encourage, too.

"You're going to lead the league in passing," he said to Lamar McHan.

"You're my top runner," he said to "Golden Boy" Paul Hornung.

"When your coach talks to you that way," said quarterback McHan, "you've got to play great ball."

Bart Starr would have to wait forever, or so it seemed to him, that first year with Lombardi, for even the slightest of kind words. As a matter of fact, he was in for a few harsh moments before he was to experience anything like approval from his coach.

Green Bay had been the unanimous choice of the nation's football writers to end the season at the bottom of the league when the writers made their preseason predic-

tions in 1959. They all were astonished when the
Packers defeated the Chicago Bears, 9–6, in the opening
game of the season.

"Surprise Victory for Green Bay," is the way they
headlined their stories.

There was great joy in Green Bay with this opening
win of the Packers, and the win undoubtedly gave the
team a lift. But there was no personal joy for Bart Starr
in the victory. He had played only a few minutes and in
his one effort to throw a pass he had been rushed, battered, and thrown for an 8-yard loss.

The Packers won their second game, and their third
game, but Bart had little if anything to do with the victories. Nor did he do anything in the next four games
which Green Bay lost to the Baltimore Colts, the New
York Giants, in its second meeting with them, the Chicago Bears, and again to the Baltimore Colts.

The Giant game provided a real downer for Bart.
Quarterback McHan was hurt.

Lombardi looked at his bench, and Bart Starr readied
himself to jump into the battle. After all, at that time,
he considered himself the backup quarterback.

But Lombardi wasn't sending him in.

"Francis!" he barked, and Joe Francis, Number Three
quarterback, was off and running.

Bart Starr said nothing, covering up the sinking feeling in the pit of his stomach. The coach, he reasoned,
doesn't have even enough confidence to send me in
when we're losing.

"Go to it, Joe!" he yelled after Francis, as the quarterback moved onto the playing field. "Show 'em!"

Bart was hurt, and he was hurt badly. For all purposes he was a failure.

"Failure. Failure. Failure."

The word kept running in his mind, and he began to wonder when he ought to pack his things and just go home.

The turn in Bart's fortunes, however, was not far off. In the losing battle against the Colts, Bart started the game and immediately moved the Packers. Bart passed to Jim Taylor for 20 yards and a touchdown. There was something about the determined way that Bart took the Packers down to the Colt goal line and over it that caught Lombardi's eye.

"Maybe I should play him more. He looks good," mused the coach. "He needs more seasoning."

Whatever the case, with the stands in Green Bay packed with the wildly fanatic Packer rooters for the last Green Bay game at home against the Washington Redskins, Lombardi didn't hesitate to send Bart Starr in the game, to replace a faltering Lamar McHan. And Bart was outstanding.

Starr passed nineteen times in that game, and eleven of those passes were successful. He spotted a weakness in the defense and had his backs running through the big holes. He mixed up his plays wisely, and had Washington constantly off balance. He was the key man of the Green Bay offense as the Packers won the game, 24–0.

"That's the way to play the game," said Coach Lombardi, laconically.

It was the Detroit Lions next, and again it was a

more confident Bart Starr, completing 10 of his 15 passes for 169 yards, who keyed a victory for the Packers, 24–17.

"The most important thing is consistent execution," said Lombardi, and he must have been thinking of Bart's consistency. "Consistent execution wins the ball games."

Against the Los Angeles Rams—the team that had whipped them so badly earlier in the season—Bart passed to rookie Boyd Dowler for 2 touchdowns. He did something else that must have pleased Lombardi no end. Twice he called for a play that fooled the Rams. Bart took the pass from center, lateraled the ball to Paul Hornung far to his right, and Paul promptly tossed the ball down the field to Dowler and 2 more touchdowns for the high-flying Green Bay Packers.

Packers, 38; Rams, 20. Bart Starr was finally coming into his own. For the moment he was Number One quarterback for the Green Bay Packers, and it seemed that all his perseverance and drive and determination had finally paid off. All the bitter, frustrating years were now seemingly at an end.

Against the San Francisco Forty-niners Bart was brilliant, leading the Packers to a 36–14 victory. He passed 25 times, connected with 20, bewildering the Forty-niner defense as he hit six different receivers for a most impressive 249 yards. It was his greatest day in pro football.

For the Green Bay Packers it was a successful season. For the first time since 1946 they finished the year with a winning percentage and only 2 games behind the champion Baltimore Colts.

For Vince Lombardi it was a fine season. In his first year as a head coach of a professional football team, he had turned the Green Bay Packers around, fashioned a winner out of a perennial loser.

For Bart Starr, the year of 1959 had begun as close as anything could be to disaster, but had ended in a blaze of personal glory. Lombardi had sent him in to quarterback the team after it had lost four straight and, he had quarterbacked the team brilliantly to four straight victories. Victories on the gridiron are team victories, of course, but if anyone were to name the star of those four victories with which Green Bay closed its season, it would have to be Bart Starr.

Nobody read that in the sports pages that year because nobody wrote it. The eyes of the sportswriters were on Paul Hornung, Jim Taylor, Boyd Dowling, and, of course, Vincent Lombardi. And these were the men whose names monopolized the stories they wrote about the Green Bay Packers' amazing turn-around. It was going to take them some time yet to catch up with and recognize the potential of the young Packer quarterback.

The closing games of the 1959 season had demonstrated how capable Bart Starr was. He would carve his name in the Football Hall of Fame in years to come. In 1960, however, he was still to suffer moments of discouragement before he was to lead the Green Bay Packers once more to victory.

CHAPTER 13

"Starting at quarterback for the Packers . . . Bart Starr . . ."

The announcer's voice boomed through City Stadium in Green Bay. In the preseason games, Bart had moved the Packers. Now and at last he was the Number One quarterback in the Packers' 1960 opening game—against the Chicago Bears.

On the sideline, Bart warmed up, tossing short passes to teammate Paul Hornung. He could feel the tension building up inside, pinching his stomach. His hands were wet, and his knees were just a bit shaky. He was opening the season as the quarterback for the team. After all the gloomy, heartbreaking years of frustration and disappointment, here at last was his chance for recognition.

Suddenly he stopped short, turned his head for a fleeting glimpse of Cherry in the stands. He spotted her dressed in an attractive green-and-gold coat. She stood up and waved at him and Bart suddenly felt loose and comfortable.

He trotted out onto the playing field as the big crowd

of some 55,000 Green Bay partisans roared. After the opening kickoff, Bart steered the Packers artfully down the field, mixing his passes and running plays, moving the Packers to the Bears' 30-yard line. But the Bears, full of fight, stiffened and held. Somehow, Starr couldn't pull off the magic play that would spring someone loose for a touchdown, and the Bears took the ball over on downs. Only twice was Bart Starr able to lead his men across the Chicago goal line for 2 touchdowns, and that wasn't enough. The final score of the game was Chicago, 17; Packers, 14.

It was a bitter loss for Green Bay. It was worse for Bart Starr. Vince Lombardi called on Lamar McHan to quarterback the Packers in their second game of the season, against the Detroit Lions.

Bart sat on the bench, disheartened, as he watched McHan call the signals. But McHan wasn't doing well, the Packers were ineffective, and Bart forgot his disappointment as his fingers began to itch for the ball.

"I can move them," thought Bart, with growing impatience; but he said nothing.

It was Vince Lombardi who did the saying.

"Get in there, Starr! Move 'em!"

And that's what Bart Starr did.

Run. Pass. Run. Starr was a brilliant field general as he directed the team down the field. He sent Jim Taylor through the middle of the Detroit line for one touchdown. He sent Paul Hornung off-tackle for another. The game became a romp for the Packers, and they whipped the Lions by the score of 28–9.

Lombardi was not yet convinced who should be his

Number One quarterback. Or maybe he was employing some kind of psychology to psyche Bart. Whatever the case, he started the third game of 1960 with Lamar McHan again at quarterback, against Johnny Unitas, the legendary quarterback of the world champion Baltimore Colts.

However, as he had done against the Detroit Lions, Coach Lombardi yanked Lamar early in the game and sent in Bart once more. Whatever way he had planned it, whatever he may have had in mind, it was a great psychological move on the part of Lombardi for the team, and a vote of confidence for Bart Starr.

For a while it was a duel between two men who are generally considered among the very best who ever called signals on the football field. But Starr pulled his team ahead and Johnny Unitas and the Colts just couldn't catch up with them. The Packers walked off the gridiron jubilant with a hard-fought 35–21 victory, and Vince Lombardi called Starr into his office.

"I want you to know I made a mistake here," said Lombardi. "We've been drifting back and forth, shuttling you and McHan in and out of the game, and I realize what it's done to you. I want to tell you right now that there aren't going to be any more changes. You are going to be my quarterback, and I don't want you to worry about anything or anybody else, but the game plan. Now let's get this team on the road! Right, Bart?" Lombardi grinned as he finished speaking and then as Bart turned to go, Lombardi clapped him smartly on the back.

"You're it," the coach said to his quarterback. "From

now on, you're Number One. You don't have to worry about a thing."

"Thank you, sir," said Bart, and Lombardi just stared at the young man.

He remembered saying that he thought Bart Starr was just too polite a man, too self-effacing, to be the authoritarian leader football seems to demand of its quarterbacks. Yet here was the son of an Army master-sergeant, with all the courtesy and discipline common to Army men and Army life, who could move the battle-toughened Packer squad down the field with precision, and to victory.

But Bart was tough, too, for all his gentle manners, as both Lombardi and the Green Bay Packers were soon to learn. Around the league, and even among his own men, Starr was considered something of a "pussycat." The general opinion was he was a little on the polite side and not tough enough. It was even thought that, when it came to a showdown, he would be short on sheer "guts." They were as far off the mark as they could possibly be, and, in the second meeting of the Chicago Bears and the Packers in 1960, Bart Starr was going to turn all that kind of negative thinking around.

It was early in the game. Bill George, one of the Bears' great linebackers, red-dogged, punched a hole in the line, and came right at Bart, hit him in the mouth, cut his lip and knocked him down.

Bill George didn't offer his hand to help the quarterback up on his feet. He just stood there for a moment, watching the blood trickle out of Bart Starr's mouth.

"I'll take care of you, Starr!" he whistled. "You're a pussycat!"

Bart got up on his feet, spit the blood out of his mouth, then had a few words for Bill George.

"You——!"

Jerry Kramer says, "That was the first time I ever heard Bart Starr swear. It was the last time, too."

Vince Lombardi was for pulling Bart out of the game, to stitch the cut in his mouth. But Bart would have none of it. After all it was Lombardi who had said, "You've got to learn to play even when you hurt." Bart would play with injuries worse than a cut mouth, a whole lot worse, and conceal those injuries from his coach and teammates, too.

He didn't say a word in the huddle. He just directed the next play, right at Bill George and the next, and the next. The Packers just walked all over the Chicago Bears that afternoon and came home with a 41–13 victory.

They came home with something else that afternoon. No one, just no one, could ever tell them again that Bart Starr, the man who wouldn't drink more than a beer, or smoke, or cuss, the man who never had a harsh word for anybody on the field or off it, the man who was always saying, "Yes, sir," and "No, sir," was not mentally tough. For once and forever, Bart Starr had demonstrated to his teammates—and to his opposition as well—that he had the guts a football player must have to play the game.

Bart led his team to eight victories in the 1960 season and the Western Conference championship in the National League. He called plays brilliantly. His passing was phenomenal. He threw 172 passes in 1960, completed 98 of them for an average of 57 per cent. Four of those passes went for touchdowns, and he was intercepted but 8 times. The sportswriters suddenly began to take note of the Packer quarterback and occasionally penned a few words about his prowess, but not much. Bart wasn't a sensational player. He was a team player, out there to do a job, and doing it well. He wasn't the glamour boy who makes the headlines. He was the efficient quarterback who brought home the victories.

"He's not a Johnny Unitas," was what one heard from both the writers and the fans. "He can't throw the long bomb. He doesn't gamble. You always know the play he's going to call. Besides, he always has Paul Hornung and Jim Taylor to make him look like a smart quarterback."

It wasn't too bad being compared with Johnny Unitas of the Baltimore Colts, one of the greatest of all time. It was true, too, that the running of Hornung and Taylor were among the Packers' greatest assets. But it was Starr who called the plays. It was Starr who passed with a brilliance and almost pin-point accuracy. Bart Starr had all of the necessary attributes of one of football's greatest quarterbacks right from the start, but it was going to take a long time before the fans and the sportswriters recognized it.

Bart led his team the day after Christmas, 1960, to do battle with the Philadelphia Eagles, winners of the Eastern Conference crown of the National League, for the football championship of the world. The Packers were flying high. The Western Conference title was the first championship Green Bay had won in sixteen years. There was determination in the ranks, inspired to a fighting pitch by coach Vince Lombardi, to leave Philadelphia, where the world championship game was to be played, and return home to Green Bay as world champions.

Starr had a worthy opponent in the brilliant Eagle quarterback, Norm Van Brocklin. The Packer defense, with men like Jerry Kramer and Ray Nitschke, was formidable. So was the Eagle defense, led by the great Chuck Bednarik. It promised to be a great game, a dramatic struggle, and the contest lived up to all that was expected of it.

Two field goals by Paul Hornung gave the Packers a 6–0 lead early in this bitterly fought game. It was going to be a relatively low-scoring battle with few touchdowns. The Eagles, however, did get into the Packer end zone once in the first half of the game and, coupled with a field goal, led Green Bay by the score of 10–6 at the halfway mark.

With both clubs playing magnificent defensive football, the score was still 10–6 going into the fourth and final quarter. Then, abruptly, dramatically, Bart Starr began to find his passing eye. Despite the thick fog that was settling on the Philadelphia gridiron, he hit Max McGee on the Eagle 45-yard line. He passed to Paul Hornung on the Eagle 20. Two running plays and the Green Bay Packers were on the Philadelphia 13.

Third down and 3 to go, Bart took the pass from center, stepped back into his protective pocket, looked down the field, spotted Ron Kramer, the great ex-Michigan star, all alone, on the goal line, whipped the ball to him, and Kramer caught the pigskin precisely on the goal line, and fell over it into the Eagle end zone. Touchdown!

It was the first time that afternoon that the Packers had been able to move across the Eagle's goal line and, with only 5 minutes to play, it looked like Green Bay was about to achieve the "impossible dream." The Packers kicked off, holding a 13–10 lead, but the Eagle rookie, Ted Dean, returned that kick-off brilliantly, all the way down to the Green Bay 39-yard line.

Norm Van Brocklin took charge. He took his time. He was confident that the Eagles could score against a tiring Packer team, but he wanted to eat up as much time as he could. He didn't want to give Bart Starr another chance to snatch victory out of defeat.

Van Brocklin took three and a half minutes moving the Eagles down to the Green Bay goal line and into its end zone, and it was Ted Dean who moved in from the 5-yard line for the Philadelphia TD which put them in command, 17–13.

There were just ninety seconds on the clock, when Bart Starr took the ball for the last time that afternoon, on its own 20-yard line. Eighty yards is a long way to go in 90 seconds.

A short pass and a short gain. Another short pass and another short gain, as each time the receiver stepped out of bounds to stop the clock. But time can't be stopped forever, and the Packers found themselves just inside the Eagles' 20-yard line with time for one final play of the game.

The Packers knew what they had to do. The play had been called. Everyone knew it had to be a desperation pass, a pass for a score. Everyone had his assignment.

Bart took the snap from center, moved back quickly, found Jim Taylor on the 9-yard line, whipped the ball to him. Taylor gathered in the pigskin, lunged toward the goal line; but there was Chuck Bednarik, smashing into him, holding him and, with three more big Philadelphia linemen to help, bore him down to the ground.

The game was over. The Philadelphia Eagles were world champions.

"Almost," said Kramer in the locker room, after the game.

"Not good enough," said Bart Starr.

He was a competitor. Like Vince Lombardi, he believed that winning was everything.

After the game, Coach Lombardi, very deliberate in his message, said, "Perhaps you men didn't realize that you could have won this game. But I don't think there's any doubt in your minds now. And that's why you will win the world's championship next year."

CHAPTER 14

Early in January and February of 1961 Bart Starr heard a number of disquieting rumors. According to some sportswriters, Vince Lombardi was very unhappy about losing the world championship in 1960 to the Philadelphia Eagles. There was much talk about the Packer coach shopping around for a more experienced quarterback. Specifically, or so the stories had it, he was maneuvering for a trade for Don Meredith, the brilliant quarterback of the Dallas Cowboys. According to the grapevine, Vince Lombardi was ready to give Dallas any two players on the Green Bay Packer roster, and more for the Cowboy he wanted to lead his club in 1961.

Considering the outstanding year Bart had had, considering the fact that he had led the Packers to its first championship in sixteen years, Bart had reason to be discouraged and bewildered.

"I thought I gave it everything I had," he said, in the presence of his most intimate companions. "I thought I did a pretty good job."

But he said nothing publicly, and nothing for the

press. He respected Lombardi too much to question his coach's moves, as reported in the sports pages anyway.

"It couldn't have been because I asked for too big a pay hike?" he mused, speaking to his wife in the privacy of their home.

At the end of the 1960 season Bart had walked into Lombardi's office to discuss his contract for the 1961 season.

Lombardi had been after Bart to be more aggressive, to be less self-effacing, mild-mannered.

"You've got to be tough," said Lombardi to all of his men.

"You've got to be tough," he had hammered, especially at his quarterback, and all season.

Bart, walking into Lombardi's office that afternoon, to talk contract, decided that that was exactly what he was going to be: tough, firm, aggressive. And aggressively he confronted Lombardi with the terms he wanted in his 1961 contract.

"I was probably overfirm," says Bart Starr, "trying to compensate for usually being meek and mild in front of him."

Lombardi had listened to his quarterback's demands, leaned back in his chair, and exploded.

"You think you're worth it?" he had demanded.

"Yes, sir," came back Bart, politely but firmly.

"A fine time to become the tough guy!" yelled the coach.

"You want me to be tough, Mr. Lombardi. That's what you've been hitting me with all season, sir."

The "sir" was always there.

Lombardi had looked at the young quarterback, not knowing exactly how to react.

"My God!" he had finally said. "I've created a Frankenstein!"

"I had to laugh," says Bart, "and Mr. Lombardi began to laugh, too."

But Bart Starr never said whether Lombardi had ever met his salary demands in the coach's office that afternoon after the last game of the 1960 season.

"I am his creation," Bart would say of Vince Lombardi. "I literally owe my life to that man, both on and off the field."

It was Starr's intense feeling for his coach that had him so disturbed in the first months of 1961. And it wasn't until late in March of that year that he got word that his position with the Green Bay Packers was firm—the assurance he needed so badly.

First, the rumors about Vince Lombardi looking for a trade with Dallas and the acquisition of Don Meredith slowly died and disappeared from the sports pages. If Meredith had been acquired, he would have become undoubtedly the Number One quarterback for the Packers, and Bart Starr would have been demoted to backup man. That wasn't going to happen now. Now, the only question unresolved for both Green Bay and Bart was whether Lamar McHan could come back to challenge Bart for that Number One spot. Lamar had had more years in professional football, more experience. If he showed his old-time form, he would be the Packers' logical choice for the starting line-ups.

But late in March Bart got word that Lamar McHan

had been traded to the Washington Redskins, and this was particularly good news for the young quarterback. First, it meant that Vince Lombardi had made up his mind about his Number One man: Bart Starr. Second, and perhaps more importantly at the moment, Vince Lombardi had given his young quarterback his vote of confidence. It was his confidence that needed building, in Bart's first years as a professional gridder, and Vince Lombardi was immeasurably helpful helping him build it.

"If I threw an interception," Bart says, "even in training camp, I'd fret about it. I'd brood, if I thought I had made a bad call."

Brooding and fretting do nothing for a player's morale. On the contrary, they dampen the spirit and cut into confidence.

As the 1960 season had progressed, Bart had become less and less worried by his occasional errors. He had learned to take an interception in stride, as something that happens with the best of quarterbacks. The best of quarterbacks make bad calls every now and then.

"The thing to do is to rectify the error," says Bart. "You don't let a mistake get you down. You do something about it."

It was with this spirit that Bart Starr led the Packers to victory in all its five preseason games against league competition. The sportswriters were predicting that Green Bay would repeat, winning its second Western Conference title in two years. There were a good many sportswriters, too, who were of the opinion that the

Packers would go all the way and rack up the world championship of football in that season of 1961.

The season opened, however, inauspiciously for the Packers lost their first encounter in 1961 to the Detroit Lions by the score of 17–13. The Lions ripped apart the Green Bay defense, and knocked down Starr again and again. There was something ominous about that kind of repetition, and there was no question about the resolve it put into the Packer squad.

Bart went back to Green Bay and spent an entire day studying the films of the game. He would always study the movies of the game. He studied the plays that had worked well, and why they had worked well. He studied the plays that had gone wrong, and why. The Packers' blocking had broken down in that first game of the season, against the Lions; Detroit had blitzed, and blitzed again, breaking down the Packer passing game. He studied that blitz, noted how and why the Lions defensive team had ripped up the center of the Packer line.

"Out on the field," said Vince Lombardi of his quarterback, "he knows what's going on with the other team's defense. He knows it better than any of the coaches."

This was the year when such Packer stars as Paul Hornung, Rookie of the Year Boyd Dowler and the powerful linebacker Ray Nitschke were ordered to report for Army service. They managed one way and another to get weekend passes to play in the championship games, but they consistently missed the important mid-week drills and practice. This was the year that Jerry Kramer suffered a separated ankle in the second game of the season and when team captain Jim Ringo was twice hospitalized with a painful case of the boils. But the team played on, and following that first defeat, walloped the Forty-niners by the score of 30–10; shut out the Chicago Bears, 24–0; romped over the Baltimore Colts, 45–7; took Cleveland, 49–17; and the Minnesota Vikings twice, 33–7 and 28–10.

In the Cleveland game, Bart suffered a strained abdominal muscle, a painful injury. For the next five games, he was injected with a pain killer, but he played and played brilliantly. There was little mention of his injury in the sports pages. Bart didn't advertise it. And the way he ran his ball club and threw the ball, no one in the stands could know what pain the young quarterback suffered during the sixty minutes on the gridiron.

Green Bay just bulled its way through its opposition in the regular schedule of the 1961 season, won 11 of its 14 games and easily came out on top of its division in the National Football League. For the second time in two years, the Packers were the champions of the Western Conference. The New York Giants, with their two ace quarterbacks, Charlie Conerly and Y. A. Tittle—the Gray Fox and the Bald Eagle, as they were called in New York; with Sam Huff, that superb linebacker; with two of the fastest men in the league, Dick Lynch and Jim Patton as a protective umbrella against the pass, had taken the Eastern Conference title. The battle between these two great teams for the world title in football promised to prove a bruising and dramatic struggle.

Green Bay went wild in the anticipation of the game. The talk in all the bars, the restaurants, the stores, the streets, was that Green Bay was going to run the Giants into the ground, cut them down to size. So sure were the townspeople of Green Bay that they were going to boast the championship of the football world that they had signs printed, reading, "Titletown, U.S.A." and plastered the sign on every available door, wall, and window.

The Giants came to Green Bay prepared to stop the off-tackle slants of Paul Hornung and Jim Taylor. In fact, the entire Giant defense was keyed to stop Taylor. The Giants knew that Paul Hornung had been in the Army most of the last half of the season. Paul did not figure to be running with his usual sharpness. To make Green Bay's chances even gloomier, Jimmy Taylor was limping on a battered leg. When the game started, Allie Sherman, the Giant coach, surprised the Packers with an unusual defense—a five-man front line. Twice Starr sent Taylor and Hornung smashing into that five-man line, and twice the two big backs were stopped for little or no gain.

In the huddle Starr called out the play. On the snap from center, Bart spun and handed off to Hornung. Two Packer guards pulled out of the line to lead the way for Hornung, and Paul streaked out into the open and was almost in the clear when a Giant safetyman caught him from behind with a great tackle.

Despite that fine run for 25 yards by Hornung, the Giants were still readying their defense to stop the smashing charges by Jimmy Taylor.

But Bart had other ideas. "Taylor was hurt, so he wasn't going to be effective. Then Hornung had looked so good in our workouts. Even though he had missed a lot of practice, he was running good. I made up my mind—and I'm sure Coach Lombardi felt the same way —that I'd use Paul a lot more."

In the first period Henry Jordan, the veteran Dave Hanner, and Bill Quinlan stopped the vaunted Giant running game. Willie Davis was a demon at end, rushing the New York quarterback, forcing Y. A. Tittle to hurry his passes. The Giants could go nowhere. But neither could the Packers until Starr began to find the range and in the last minutes of the first quarter drove straight downfield 74 yards to the Giants' 6-yard line as the gun ended the first period.

The second period of that championship game was one that Green Bay Packer fans will never forget.

Right from the gun, the Giants were keying on Jim Taylor, and watched his every move. Bart Starr had watched the Giant linebacker Sam Huff move to the right of the line. He realized that Sam was there to stop Taylor's off-tackle slant, and on the snap from center Bart faked handing the ball to Taylor, then spun to his right and handed the ball to Paul Hornung, and Paul blasted through the left side of the Giant line and raced into the end zone for a TD. A Hornung boot, and the score was Green Bay, 7; New York, 0.

A Nitschke interception, a toss from Bart Starr to Boyd Dowler, and 4 minutes later the score was Packers, 14; Giants, 0.

Another intercepted pass, this time by Hand Gremminger and then Bart on successive plays sending Taylor and Hornung into the line, moved the Packers to the

Giants' 14. From there, Starr passed to Ron Kramer for the third TD of the quarter.

With time running out on the half, Starr, equal again to the task, engineered another Packers' drive from their own 6-yard line to where Paul Hornung booted a field goal and 3 more points for Green Bay, just as the gun went off.

In the third quarter, Bart tossed another TD pass, hitting Ron Kramer in the New York end zone. The Giants were a thoroughly beaten team. They couldn't break through that Packer line. Their quarterbacks were rushed, and twice Jess Whittenton intercepted Y. A. Tittle passes. Herb Adderley intercepted another.

There were two more field goals Hornung kicked that afternoon and Green Bay ran off the field champions of the football world, to the roar of the deliriously happy Green Bay fans.

In the clubhouse there were tears and cheers.

"Bart Starr performed like a champion," said Vince Lombardi.

Champion, indeed! He had completed 10 of his 17 passes, 3 for touchdowns. Not one of his passes had been intercepted.

"Starr called the plays," said Lombardi. "He made the right calls, changed the plays at the line when he had to. He knows exactly what to do, and he does it!"

Strange, however, for all of Vince Lombardi's praise, for all the coach's recognition of the great play of his quarterback, the sportswriters' eyes were not on Bart Starr that afternoon of the Packers' great victory.

They cornered Lombardi, of course. They interviewed

Hornung and Taylor and Jim Ringo and almost every-body else on the Green Bay squad.

"The key man for us was Bart Starr," said an assistant coach, but Bart sat on a stool, alone, and away from the host of sportswriters who jammed the clubhouse.

Just one, and only one, of the writing crew displayed any interest in the young hero.

"How does it feel," he asked the tired Starr, "to out-smart two old pros like Conerly and Tittle?"

Bart replied quickly.

"We won as a team. We have no individual stars in Green Bay. I didn't try to match wits with the Giant quarterbacks. No, sir. The team won this game."

CHAPTER 15

Perhaps the sportswriters and, for the most part, the fans all over the country had yet to recognize the greatness of Bart Starr. Not so the city in which he was born, Montgomery, Alabama.

There, on January 17, 1962, the city of Montgomery celebrated "Bart Starr Night," and almost everybody who had had anything to do with Bart as a young boy growing up in that wonderful, gracious southern city was there to do him honor.

Bill Mosely, who had coached Starr at Sidney Lanier High School in Montgomery, was the master of ceremonies.

"With a fellow like Bart on your team," he said, "it was just as if you had a coach in the game. We coaches didn't make Bart a good player. He made us good coaches."

Red Drew, Bart's coach at Alabama declared, "Bart Starr was the best passer I ever coached."

Bill Chandler, director of Montgomery's YMCA program, said, "Bart Starr is a golden example for all our young boys. We are happy that he is a product of

Montgomery, and we are glad that he had a part in our program over the years."

Florian Strassburger, president of the Montgomery Boys Club, echoed those sentiments. "Bart Starr is an inspiration for our youngsters and we are happy for them that he has reached the top in sports."

Nick Germanos, who had played with Starr at Lanier and Alabama, added a light touch.

"I knew Bart Starr," he said, "when he used that kid stuff on his hair.

"Seriously," continued Germanos, "Bart is one of the finest all-around men I have ever been associated with. And that's why he's a great football player. He plays the game of life clean all the way, and that's why he has been successful."

The main speaker of that evening, of course, was the guest of honor, and in the speech he made for his hometown people, Bart Starr revealed a talent he had been able to conceal from everybody for a long, long time.

"When we won the National Football League championship," he began, "I thought at the moment that was my biggest thrill. But the fine welcome, seeing my old Lanier High School coach, Bill Mosely, my great friends Bobby Barnes and Nick Germanos, who played with me at Lanier and then at Alabama, and then to see Coach Drew, and the nice things that have happened here, and were said to me during my three-day stay in my home town is really the greatest thrill I'll ever have, and I thank every one of you from the bottom of my heart."

Spoken in Bart's soft voice and soft Southern drawl, it moved everyone assembled to honor him.

It was in this after-dinner speech, too, that Bart listed his "key to success," a list of qualities essential "to reach the goal you're aiming for." First came preparation, then practice, perseverance, desire, thinking you can win, prayer, and a good sense of humor.

"It takes them all to succeed," said Bart, "in just about anything that you undertake in this present-day life."

Bart Starr was scheduled to make a lot of after-dinner speeches. He learned how to capture and hold an audience. He knew how to appeal to the "inner man" by relating stories of courage and inspiration. He even became a master at telling the funny story—a funny story, however, with a happy ending and something that would give a boost to the morale of his listeners.

He would tell, for example, about the one game the Packers lost in its 1962 season, to the Detroit Lions.

"They almost took our heads off before we even got out on the field," he says.

"There was a time out. It was late in the third period and the Lions had the game already safely won.

"What do you think about a sweep around right end?" Bart asked his teammate, Tom Moore. "Pick up a first down?"

Moore swallowed hard. "Eight yards on a run?" he queried. "McCord has been killing me every time I try that sweep. Why don't you give the ball to Taylor?"

Taylor shook his head.

"Run for eight yards inside? Not with the way Roger Brown has been hitting me. I'm sore all the way up and down, from my head to my cleats. Why not a pass?"

"They had been blitzing all afternoon," says Bart. "I'd been rushed and knocked down so much, my bones ached thinking about it."

"What about a pass, Boyd?"

Boyd Dowler became philosophical.

"I'd like to help," he said, "but Night Train Lane has my ribs all sore. He's there every time I get near the ball. How about throwing the ball to McGee?"

"Max McGee," says Bart, "started to edge toward the side lines and was almost off the field by the time Boyd Dowler got through with his speech."

"It was Fuzzy Thurston," says Bart, "who came up with the best idea, I guess."

Fuzzy had been taking his lumps in the line that day, particularly from the Lions' Roger Brown.

"Why don't you throw a long incomplete pass?" said Fuzzy Thurston. "Then nobody will get hurt."

Of course the story, repeated often at the many dinners and banquets attended as guest of honor, drew a big laugh. But Bart wasn't satisfied with just a laugh. He had to point up a moral.

"I told you this story," he would say, "not only because it's human and funny, but because it's about a football player holding on to his sense of humor in a crisis."

Phil Bengtson, Lombardi's assistant coach at the time of this incident, recalls it vividly.

"I remember the incident," Bengtson says. "They were all laughing out there on the field like a bunch of school kids. There were fifty-eight thousand fans in the

Detroit stands, just gaping, completely puzzled by what was going on on the gridiron."

"What have they got to laugh about?" they asked each other. "They're having their tails whipped, and they're laughing!"

The players on the bench, both benches, were no less puzzled by the strange antics of the Packers in one of their zany moments.

CHAPTER 16

Coach Vince Lombardi stood up in the clubhouse. The Packer squad, suited up for their first day of the 1962 practice season, watched him intently as he started to speak. The coach looked around at his players. "This is going to be a very tough year for us," he barked. "This year every team in the league is going to be keyed up to beat us. We won the Western Conference title in 1960, again in 1961. Nobody can take that away from us. But a lot of teams—the Giants, Lions, Bears, Colts—are going to go all out, do their level best to beat us this season."

Lombardi stared at his players, paused, "Are you going to let them take that championship away from us?"

"No!" roared his players. A few more statements from Lombardi and they charged out onto the practice field for the first practice session of the 1962 season.

Later that afternoon, after a strenuous practice session, Bart Starr sat in front of his locker. Sweat poured down his face, and he looked tired, but he was happy and began to talk.

"The great thing about Coach Lombardi," he said, "is that he really prepares you for each and every game. He repeats, drills, drills, repeats, until finally you can recognize the other team's various defenses in your sleep. Coach gives you the confidence you've got to have going into a game."

Bart was confident as he waited for the opening kickoff of the 1962 season. He was nervous as usual as he waited on the side line for the kick to start the game. On the opposite side of the field, the Minnesota Vikings warmed up. And in the stands more than 55,000 Green Bay fans thundered applause as each Packer was introduced.

Minnesota kicked off and Green Bay took over. In the huddle Starr called the first play, moved up to the line of scrimmage with his teammates. He stood there quietly for a long second, scanning the Viking defense. He felt the tension up in his chest and his hands were moist with perspiration. Then he took the snap from center Jim Ringo, and handed the ball to Jim Taylor. He heard the crack! crack! crack! as the defense charged Taylor, the yells and grunts of the players as they drove into each other, savagely, their cleats pounding the turf. He looked up to watch Taylor fall to the ground after taking three Vikings with him, but not before he picked up 5 yards on the play. And then suddenly he felt all the tension drain off and he was the calm, efficient, clever quarterback of the champion Green Bay Packers—on their way to one of the greatest years in the history of Green Bay football.

Paul Hornung was voted the Most Valuable Player in

the National Football Leauge in 1961, and it was Hornung starting in where he had left off the previous season, running wild against the Vikings. All Paul did was to score 3 touchdowns, kick 4 field goals, and 3 conversions for a total of 33 points. Starr directed the team in flawless style, and 2 of Hornung's touchdowns came on passes by Bart Starr.

The following week the Detroit Lions put up a terrific struggle against the onrushing Packers, and once again Hornung booted 3 field goals in a 9–7 Packer win.

In the Lions' dressing room after the game, captain Joe Schmidt of the Lions shook his head. "That Bart Starr," he said. "He's so cool out there. Nothing ever seems to get to him. You can't get him mad, and that's what we like to do. Get the quarterback upset or mad. You can hit that Starr as hard as you can, he never seems to lose his poise."

The Packers continued to roll under Starr's masterful direction. The following week Elijah Pitts scored two touchdowns and Jim Taylor ran for 126 yards as they defeated Chicago, 49–0. The victory was a costly one for the Packers as Hornung was carried off the field with a severe muscle injury.

Even without the services of Hornung, Starr had the Packers in high gear, and by Thanksgiving Eve they were leading the Western Conference by 2 full games, had put together a nine-game winning streak and seemed unbeatable.

The big Thanksgiving Game against Detroit was played in tremendous Tiger Stadium on a blustery cold day. The first time Bart Starr got the ball and before he could start any play at all, big, burly Alex Karras and the 300-pound Roger Brown broke through the Packers' line and smashed Bart to the ground.

They got to Bart throughout the game, stopping the play, knocking him groggy with their smashing tackles. But each time Bart would get up, shake the cobwebs from his woozy head and come back for another play. The Lions roared to a 23–0 lead at the half. It was Detroit, 26; Green Bay, 0, at the end of the third quarter. Bart rallied the Packers in the final quarter and managed to punch over for 2 touchdowns, but it was not quite enough as the Lions shattered the Packers' two-year winning streak that had reached twelve straight games.

In the clubhouse after the game, a bruised and bloodied Starr smiled wanly at a sportswriter. "It was one of those games," he said. "No matter what you do, the other team is a jump ahead of you. It just wasn't our day."

The following week Green Bay ran roughshod over the Los Angeles Rams, 41–10, but Detroit also won. The Packers clung to their 1-game lead over the Lions.

The following Sunday that 1-game lead had disappeared. The Packers were playing the San Francisco Forty-niners at Kezar Stadium and at the half they were losing, 21–10. And as they trudged back to the clubhouse, the scoreboard showed that the Lions had won their game.

On the first play of the second half Starr started to connect with his passes. He hit Jimmy Taylor with a beautiful pass and Jimmy ran for a first down. Another pass. Complete! Another pass to Taylor and then a hand-off to Hornung, who drove in for the score. But the Packers still were behind, 21–17.

The Forty-niners failed to move the ball and the Packers took over with a vengeance. Starr was magnificent as he mixed his plays beautifully. A hand-off to Hornung—good for a first down. Hornung through left tackle for another first down, and cool Bart Starr throwing to Billy Howton, Hornung, and then Taylor for another touchdown, and the Packers led, 24–21. The Packers scored another TD before the end of the game to safely take a 31–21 victory. And now they were certain of at least a tie for the Western Conference title.

The next week, the final week of the season, the Packers squeaked through a rough afternoon against the Los Angeles Rams, 20–17, to win their third successive Western Conference championship.

The sportswriters were calling Coach Vince Lombardi "the super-coach," but Vince wasn't paying much attention to newsprint at the moment. He was in his office studying the game films of the New York Giants with his assistant coaches and his quarterback, Bart Starr.

"New York has a greatly improved team," said Lombardi. "We'll be playing them in Yankee Stadium and it will be tough."

"We took them last year, 37–0, coach," said Bart Starr, "and they'll be out for revenge."

Some 65,000 Giant fans, screaming for revenge, turned out for the game between the Packers, who had lost but one game all season, and the New Giants with a brilliant record of 12 victories and 2 losses. The fans carried banners titled: "Beat the Pack" and "Remember

1961." Those banners were soon frozen as the fifty-mile-an-hour sub-zero weather whipped the stadium turf, while the fans in the stands huddled, shivering under their woolen blankets and parkas.

Out on the playing field, Starr tried to warm up. He clapped his hands together, ran a few short sprints, and tried to throw a few passes, but the howling, icy wind shattered the flight of the ball. "It is not a day for a passing game," Starr said to no one in particular. "We're going to have to stay on the ground."

For most of the first period, Starr called straight-ahead running plays and power sweeps to the right or left, with Jim Taylor carrying the brunt of the attack. Big Jim bulled and crashed through the Giant defense with abandon. He simply ran right at the Giant players for those extra 3–4 much-needed yards.

Bart moved the Packers to the Giant 26-yard line and then big Ron Kramer, who had replaced the injured Paul Hornung as the Packers' place-kicker, booted the ball through the uprights for the first score of the game. Green Bay lead, 3–0. Late in the first half, Starr directed the Packers to the Giants' 7-yard line. Jimmy Taylor, bloodied and battered by the Giants' tough line play, grabbed Starr's arm before the next play.

"Give me the ball," he said.

When the ball was snapped, Bart handed it to Taylor. He charged in, head and shoulders lowered like a human battering ram, and banged right into the Giants' great linebacker, Sam Huff. Taylor hit Huff like a stampeding bull moose, knocked him down, trampled over him into the icy ground, and kept churning those pistonlike legs as he crashed over that last chalk stripe for the touch-down. Even the New York Giant fans cheered Taylor's awesome run. At the half, Green Bay led, 10–0.

All afternoon, Taylor defied the Giants. He'd get smashed to the frozen turf with half the Giant defensive team piling on top of him, and when he got up he'd turn and snarl at them, "Is that as hard as you Giants can hit?"

It looked like it was going to be another win for the Packers. The Giants constantly found themselves in a hole. Tittle couldn't find his receivers, the wind playing all sorts of crazy games with the pigskin. Y.A. threw 41 passes that afternoon and connected with only 18 of them. Bart Starr limited himself to 22 passes and con-nected 10 times, a marvelous average for the afternoon, considering the 20- and 30-mile-an-hour gusts that swept the field.

In the third quarter of that championship game, for a brief moment, it seemed that the New York fortunes had taken a change. The charge of the Giants' line, and maybe Lady Luck, made for a sudden and dramatic turn.

Jerry Kramer went back to kick for the Packers, but he never got that ball away. The Giants' all-pro Erich Barnes ripped through the Green Bay defenses, blocked Kramer's kick, and swift as a hare and hungrier, Jim Collier, the rookie New Yorker, was on the ball in the Packers' end zone. Score: Green Bay, 10; Giants, 6.

Chandler's boot made it 10–7.

The din in Yankee Stadium was enough to punch

holes in anyone's eardrums. But that was all, that afternoon, for the Giants.

Jerry Kramer kicked another field goal for the Packers, this time from the 29-yard line. Score, at the end of the third period: Packers, 13; New York, 7.

Kramer kicked another 3-pointer in the fourth period, with but 2 minutes to go, from the Giants' 30-yard line, and that was the ball game for the Green Bay Packers.

For the second year in a row now, the Green Bay Packers were champions of the football world. For the second time in two years, Bart Starr had led his team to the top of the football heap.

It had been a brilliant season. Jimmy Taylor led the league in rushing with 1,474 yards. Willie Wood led the league with 9 pass interceptions, Bart Starr led the league in passing, while his teammates, end Ron Kramer, tackle Forrest Gregg, guard Jerry Kramer, guard Fred Thurston, center Jim Ringo, fullback Jimmy Taylor, end Willie Davis, tackle Henry Jordon, linebacker Dan Currie, linebacker Bill Forestor, and halfback Herb Adderly all were named to various Press Association All-Pro teams.

There was much excitement in the press about Vince Lombardi, which he had well earned. There was much made about his "invincible" club, a title well deserved, even if it was just a bit exaggerated. There was little mention about the magnificent all-around brilliance of Bart Starr. He had none of the flashy show business attitude, color of a Paul Hornung, or the bold approach of a Jerry Kramer. He was the super-cool, calm, steady, brilliant genius who quarterbacked the Packers to one of their greatest years in history.

Bart, whatever he thought about this treatment in the press, said nothing. After all, he was a team man, and his team had won. That was good enough for him.

But Bart did say something when his team got ready to play in the annual All-Star game. He had been selected as a quarterback for the Western Division All-Star team, along with seven other Packers. He looked forward to leading those Western Division All-Stars against the East. It was the first time he had been chosen for this intersectional annual, and more than anything else at the moment, he wanted to lead the Western team to victory.

Johnny Unitas, that all-time great, however, had been selected to play with the Western All-Stars, too. This presented a sticky problem for Vince Lombardi who, because of the Packers' championship, was coach of the Western team for this particular annual event.

The question of who was the greatest quarterback in football, Bart Starr or Johnny Unitas, would consume the fans for years; still does. Vince Lombardi never did say who was the greatest quarterback in the game; that was not his problem at the moment. There were other considerations. He named Johnny Unitas as his starting quarterback for this 1962 classic.

Bart was upset.

"You're starting Unitas?" he said to Lombardi. "That's what I hear."

Lombardi waited for Bart to continue.

"I don't like it!"

"What's wrong with starting Unitas?" asked the coach, quietly.

"What's wrong?" exclaimed an angry Bart. "Don't you think I've earned the right to start the game? I've been the quarterback for the Packers for two championships! What more do you want?"

"Look," said Lombardi, trying to calm his irate quarterback, "there are eight Green Bay ballplayers on this squad. I can't start the game with all eight of them."

"I don't care how many you start with!" came back Bart Starr. "I've earned the right to quarterback the team!"

Bart's argument may have impressed his coach, but it didn't change his mind. Johnny Unitas was in there at quarterback when the East-West game began.

Bart has told this story more than once.

The first time he told it, the sportswriter commented, a little wryly, "You wouldn't have talked to Lombardi that way a couple of years ago."

"No," said Bart.

He recalled the time that Vince Lombardi accused himself of creating a Frankenstein out of his star quarterback, and he smiled.

Bart Starr was never the man to stay angry with anyone for any length of time. He has that sense of humor so necessary to carry a man through difficulties, through hardships, to ultimate victory.

As to the rivalry for first-place honors in all-time greatest quarterback, Johnny Unitas himself has said, "We're different types. Bart's an excellent quarterback, but he calls plays to control the ball. I gamble. I throw anytime. But he's a fine passer. Look at his statistics."

Bart has made no comment in this area for public consumption or the press. Privately, he thinks he is as good a quarterback as Johnny Unitas. Typical of the man, he has only praise for the great ex-star of the Baltimore Colts.

Undoubtedly, there were never two better quarterbacks in the game, and Bart Starr, at the end of 1962, still had greatness and recognition ahead of him.

CHAPTER 17

April 17, 1963, the entire football world awoke to a shocking headline in their morning papers.

HORNUNG AND KARRAS SUSPENDED INDEFINITELY

The news had not been entirely unexpected. There had been some whisperings during the season of 1962 that Pete Rozelle, Commissioner of the National Football League, had called in the FBI to check on rumors that there had been gambling among the players. There is an NFL rule that strictly prohibits betting among its players. And where there had been smoke, there was fire.

Joe Schmidt, Gary Lowe, Wayne Walker, Sam Williams and John Gordy, all of the Detroit Lions, had bet $50 each on a Green Bay win. They had never placed a bet on the outcome of a league game before, or since. Nor had they ever wagered on a game in which they had been involved. The NFL regulation, however, had been broken. They were each slapped with a $2,000 fine, and the Detroit club hit with a $4,000 fine for being lax in its supervision of its players.

Paul Hornung and Alex Karras, however, had been

somewhat more consistent betters, though they had never made bets against their own clubs—something which could never be condoned among professional athletes.

"My bets were sociable," said Paul Hornung, "with friends."

But it didn't matter to Pete Rozelle or the League. The rules had been broken. Both Karras and Hornung publicly and privately admitted they had broken the rules. There was only one course of action open to the Commissioner of professional football. Both Karras and Hornung, two of the greatest players in football, were suspended, and their suspension was indefinite.

"How long is indefinite?" the reporters asked Pete Rozelle.

"That depends on what happens from here on out," said Rozelle. "We'll be keeping our eyes on Hornung and Karras, and maybe we'll take some steps to review their cases next year."

What this meant was that the Detroit Lions were losing a star tackle and the Green Bay Packers their Golden Boy, their star runner.

Vince Lombardi felt so badly he thought of resigning his post in Green Bay when he got the final word from the Commissioner, but only for a moment.

"What are you going to do without Hornung?" asked the sportswriters, forgetting Jim Taylor was a Packer, that Tom Moore was a Packer, that there were thirty-four other Packers, and that Green Bay had the best quarterback in the league, Bart Starr.

"What are we going to do?" said Bart Starr. "We

face a tremendous challenge. No team ever has won the championship three times in a row. Coach Lombardi just has to point out the challenge to us. He knows how much we want to be the first team to win three titles in a row."

The majority of the nation's sportswriters predicted that Bart Starr would lead the Green Bay Packers to their fourth Western Conference crown in a row and their third straight National Football League championship, despite the loss of Paul Hornung.

What the writers didn't count on was the phenomenal showing of the Chicago Bears. Nor did they count on the injuries that plagued the Packers in '63, especially the injuries to their star quarterback.

Green Bay lost its first game of the season to the Bears, 10–3, but losing the season's opener was something of a habit with the Packers as they quickly shifted into high gear and racked up 8 consecutive victories over Detroit, Baltimore, the Rams, the Vikings, St. Louis, Baltimore again, the Pittsburgh Steelers, and the Minnesota Vikings. It looked like another championship for the Packers.

There were just two things wrong with the picture. The Chicago Bears were keeping pace with the Packers and were tied for the league lead; but the sheer brilliance of Bart Starr's play was suddenly halted after the Packers smashed out a 30–7 win over St. Louis. The victory was a very costly one for in that game Bart Starr's hand was broken after a particularly vicious tackle.

Bart was to be out of action for a month and it was during that month that the Packers met the Bears for their second encounter of the season. Green Bay had acquired quarterback Zeke Bratkowski from the Los Angeles club, on waivers, as soon as Bart was hurt, but neither Zeke, nor John Roach, who started at quarterback that afternoon in Chicago, could breach the Bears' defenses, and the Bears swamped the Packers in that crucial game of 1963.

Zeke Bratkowski was going to prove himself a boon to the Green Bay club. He quickly became the Number Two quarterback for the Packers and was to develop into a brilliant backup man for Bart Starr. Zeke was actually one of the very finest quarterbacks in pro football. An All-American star at Kentucky, Zeke had put in ten years as a pro quarterback, but he was good enough, modest enough, and wise enough to work so closely and efficiently with Starr that the two men became the very best personal and professional friends.

"I try to follow in my mind the pattern along Bart's mind," he said. "This goes on all the time. We live across the street from each other, and I'm at his house all the time. We work out plays on the blackboard. We look at films in Bart's den, practically every night. We're as close as any two men can possibly be."

Bart and Zeke both lived just outside the town of Green Bay. They were always in and out of each other's houses. To this day the two men and their wives and families take holidays together in Hawaii.

"The best thing about Bratkowski," said Bart Starr, reflectively, "is knowing he'll be there if I need him."

Bart came back to the football wars with just four games left on the schedule and Chicago still leading the

Western Conference. Despite the injury, the Packer quarterback was as effective as ever, and led Green Bay to a decisive 28–10 win against the San Francisco Forty-niners.

Bart was now considered the finest quarterback in the league, but he constantly worked on his game.

"Starr concentrated on his weaknesses," said Vince Lombardi of his ace, "until they became his strengths."

"He can't throw the long ball, the bomb," his critics would say and write.

Bart became a great passer of the long one, the forward pass that made for the touchdown.

"He used to throw a better turn-in to the left than to the right," said Vince Lombardi.

Bart worked on that in practice after practice with his star receiver, Herb Adderley, till, right or left, Starr was a crackerjack at it.

"He used to pull the string a little when he threw to the left," said his coach.

He learned to throw better to his left.

"Bart Starr operates like a surgeon when he's out there in the game," said Lombardi. "He is a master at diagnosing the opposition's defense, then picking it to pieces."

Bart was all that, and more. In the last four games of 1963, he took the Packers to 3 victories; the Detroit Lions held Green Bay to its only tie game of the season. And it was these same Detroit Lions who might have altered that final picture of the whole year for the battling Packers.

On the last day of the season, Chicago still led the

Western Conference, but only by the slimmest of margins. Green Bay had won 10, lost 2, tied 1. The Bears had won 11, lost 1, tied 1. A Packer victory and a Chicago loss, that final day of the football year, and both clubs would have finished in a flat-footed tie. That would have meant one more meeting between Green Bay and the Bears. With Bart Starr back in shape and healthy, it wasn't likely that Chicago could beat the Packers three times in a row in the one season. It was more than likely that Green Bay could climb to heights never attained before in professional football: champions of the Western Conference for four consecutive years, and a chance at three world championships in a row.

It wasn't to be.

Bart Starr led his team to a hard-fought victory in San Francisco that last day of the football season. Then the entire Packer squad sat glued to their televisions as the Detroit Lions, in a tie with the Chicago Bears, threatened to take that all-important game in the last seconds of the encounter. But the Bears held the Lions as the game ended, the Packers groaned in disappointment, and Chicago had won the Western Conference title.

The final standings: Chicago: 11-1-2, Green Bay: 11-2-1.

The Packers had played well enough and won enough games to come up with the championship in any ordinary season. But this had been no ordinary season. It had been a phenomenal year for the Chicago Bears, and they had well earned their crown.

That didn't make things any sweeter for Vince Lombardi who would accept nothing but winning. He would discover things even less sweet in 1964.

For Bart Starr, the broken hand, too, was a harbinger of more difficult days in the gridiron wars. His constantly improving play, the constant threat of his brilliant passing, moved the opposition to concentrate more and more on Starr. The blitz would come more often, the red-dogging would come more often, Bart Starr was going to be spilled more often and more savagely tackled. His body would pay for it, painfully.

Bart Starr, along with all his teammates, was sorely disappointed with the windup of the 1963 season. For his part, despite the broken hand and his forced absence from the playing field for more than a month, he had had an outstanding year. He had thrown 272 passes, completing 132 for 1,855 yards. Fifteen of his passes had been good for touchdowns, and his completion average for passing was 54.1 per cent.

There would be even better years for Bart Starr. But 1964 wasn't going to be one of them.

Sixty-four started off well enough. Commissioner Pete Rozelle lifted the suspension on Paul Hornung, and the Golden Boy was back in the Green Bay line-up. In the first game of the season, Bart flipped touchdown passes to Max McGee and Lenny Moore, while Paul Hornung celebrated his return to action by booting 3 field goals as the Packers walloped the Chicago Bears, 23–12. It was sweet vengeance, even if it came a bit late, for the disappointing showing against Chicago in 1963.

Paul Hornung's accurate toe, as well as his running, had been key factors in the Packers' attack during their championship years. The "Goat" was the man Lombardi had sent in for the field-goal attempts and the very important points after touchdown, and Hornung seldom missed. After that opening game in 1964, however, Paul's magic toe lost its accuracy, became undependable, and Green Bay lost three of the most important games on the 1964 schedule. The third game against the Colts was won by Baltimore, 24–21, after Paul missed 5 field-goal attempts.

To make matters worse, Jerry Kramer, the great Packer guard, was hurting badly. For a while he was in and out of the line-up.

"We'd play with broken hands," says Kramer. "We wouldn't tell Lombardi we were hurting. Never. There was something about that man that made us want to play, and we played."

"The hurt is in the mind," Lombardi would say, something he learned at his father's knees, "but Kramer isn't hurting in the mind."

The fact was that Jerry Kramer was seriously ill, that he would have to undergo a series of stomach operations. There was question about whether Kramer could ever come back into the game. He did, all right, but Lombardi didn't know it. And for the record, without a single line of publicity, that rough-and-toughest of coaches went to see Pete Rozelle to ask whether the league couldn't provide a pension for the ailing Jerry Kramer, even though he hadn't had enough years as a pro to make that pension obligatory.

For the second time in his career, Bart Starr was the

leading passer in the National Football League that year. He hit his receivers with 59.9 per cent of his passes, 15 of them for touchdowns, and he was intercepted only 4 times in the whole year. The quarterback may be the most important player in a football team, but he isn't the only player. Again, Green Bay finished second in the league standings, with a record of 8 wins against 5 losses and 1 tie.

"Always play to win," said Bart Starr at one of the many increasing number of banquets he found it necessary to attend, as a celebrity, as the guest of honor. "Winning may not be everything," he said, "but the effort put forth to win *is* everything."

He was speaking at a "Bart Starr Day" celebration, organized by the alumni of his old college, the University of Alabama.

"Any game played is worth striving to win," said Bart. "Winning often demands sacrifice. If not, the game isn't too important. Winning demands teamwork, and winning teamwork means that each member of the team perform his individual assignment to the very best of his ability."

All of these things were going to be part and parcel of Packer thinking and Packer action in 1965. Much of what Bart said he had heard from his coach, Vince Lombardi; but the ace quarterback had changed a word here and there, and brought his own meaning, out of his own experience, to his speech. "Winning is everything," Lombardi had said. The Packers of 1964 hadn't won, but they had given the game their best effort. "The *effort* put forth to win is everything," said Bart, and in his thinking, Green Bay could not be faulted for not giving its all in the season past.

"We did all we could," said Bart Starr of that disappointing year.

He wasn't looking for any excuses or offering any alibis. "Next year," he said, "we may do better."

And the Packers, with a little wise trading, and with Vince Lombardi at the helm, did do better the next year. A whole lot better. As a matter of fact, they were the best.

CHAPTER 18

It was an unusually warm day in February in Green Bay. Instead of hard-packed winter snow cuddling the landscape, there was slush—deep, sloppy, muddy slush. On his way home from school, nine-year-old Bart Starr, Jr., had to slog through the muck which oozed over the tops of his boots and made his feet wet and cold. When he came in the side door of the comfortable, spacious Starr ranch-style home in the quiet Chateau-Liberty section of Green Bay, he was in a hurry and did not think to take off his boots. As he sloshed across the rich fabric of the dining room rug, he left a thick trail of wet, dirty footprints.

Before he reached the kitchen he was seized from behind by his father, and in short order he found out that his father had a very good right arm. It was being applied with vigor to the seat of his pants, and he felt it. Cherry Starr, Bart's attractive wife, knew her eldest son was home when she heard him crying, as Bart continued to scold the boy.

After Cherry cleaned the muddy snow off the rug, she called her family in to dinner and the first thing little

Brett Starr, three years old, did was knock his glass of milk off the table—splash!

"Now that was just plain careless," said Bart to his young son. He lifted him out of the chair and paddled his backside until he, too, was in tears. Then he sent him to his room. "By the way," Bart said to Cherry. "Did you type out those letters I asked you to do for me last night?"

"Not yet," Cherry Starr said.

"Well, for gosh sakes," Starr exploded, "if I knew it was going to take you all that time I would've done it myself. You know I wanted to get them right out." He was practically sputtering.

"Now what in the world's gotten into you, Bart?" his wife said. "Hitting the children, shouting at me. What are you so jumpy about?"

Bart Starr calmed down. "Well, I got a million things to do today," he said, "and I'm running late. And I got to go over to Appelton tonight for a dinner."

"What kind of a dinner?"

"Well, they're giving me a nice-guy award."

"Bart Starr," his wife said, "you got to be kidding."

Starr, tall, blonde, with deeply set blue eyes, is the very model of a modern T-quarterback. And he tells this story as an answer to those who suggest that if he has a failing it's that he's too nice a guy.

"I'm not all that nice," he says. "Just ask Cherry." As Starr talked, seated in the comfortable downstairs den of his home, surrounded by the mementos of his football career, his older boy came into the room and showed his father a test paper from school, with a perfect score,

100. "You owe me ten cents," he said smiling. Starr dug into his pocket and handed it to the boy.

"You're going to break me," he said. The boy pocketed the coin and darted away.

Once more Bart, Jr., broke into the den. "Where's Paul Hornung?"

"He couldn't come," said Bart smiling. Hornung had been in Green Bay to visit old friends. "Paul will be here later."

Bart turned to a friend. "Paul Hornung is my son's favorite player," said Bart. "He'll cheer and yell when I complete a pass, but you should hear him yell like an Indian when Paul breaks loose on a long run."

Although Green Bay fans worship the team, they take the individual players on it rather casually. More than half of the married players have taken up permanent residence in the town, blending easily into the various neighborhoods.

One day recently Bart Starr, Jr., and several friends were shooting baskets on a court outside the Starr garage. Bart, Sr., came along and joined the game. In any other town, such a group of boys would have been speechless, but here the star quarterback was received calmly, like any other neighborhood father who wanted a game.

Bart Starr carries somewhat more weight elsewhere in Green Bay, but this is because of his civic and church activities rather than his quarterbacking. He is a board member of the First Methodist Church and serves on the Green Bay Redevelopment Authority. In recent years he has raised over $45,000 for "Rawhide, Inc." a childcare agency and summer camp for disadvantaged boys. One Green Bay shopowner tells of a personal appearance that Starr made for his store. When he asked what the fee would be, Starr told him to forget it, and instead to give a clothing certificate to a boy from a state correctional institution. Asked if a hundred dollars would be enough, Starr replied, "Just make it fifty. We won't be helping the boy if we make things come too easily for him!"

The episode is symbolic of Starr's own regime. In the tough world of pro football, he lives by a firm set of beliefs. He doesn't smoke, rarely takes a drink, and will not allow his name to be used in cigarette or liquor advertising. If occasionally he raises his voice to emit a forceful "hell" or "damn," it is probably because he is really angry. Yet his seriousness is balanced by an ease of manner, a quick, pleasant smile, unfailing good manners, and thoughtfulness of others.

Says his former teammate Paul Hornung, "Bart is a unique example of the nice guy finishing first."

If one had to describe Bart Starr's total personality, the words that come to mind are modesty, will, intelligence, pride, determination, and courtly politeness. There are times when he seems rather a goodie-goodie, but this is deceptive. He is not, for one example, a member of the Fellowship of Christian Athletes, although he keeps a Bible beside his bed and is willing to match the depth of his faith with any man's.

For all his strong feelings, Starr seems to go through life trying to offend no one. He says that on the football field, "I'll knock your head off if I have to. I wasn't always like that, but I am now." Off the field, however, he remains the nice guy he always seems.

"To Bart Starr's neighbors," wrote Len Wagner, a sportswriter for the Green Bay *Press-Gazette*, "he's the guy who, along with Cherry, his wife, joins the neighborhood gang for a summer Sunday afternoon picnic. He's the guy who offers you the use of his lawn tools when you find yourself confronted with a sticky project. He's the guy who calls to see if your daughter can babysit Saturday night."

Robert Stewart and his famous neighbor occasionally stop on the street or meet in their living rooms to have long talks. "I've had a couple of real serious discussions with Bart," Stewart was saying, "but I'd rather not talk about it. Our discussions were private."

All of the boys in the neighborhood know who Bart Starr is. During the football season they watch him from the grandstand of Green Bay City Stadium, and they cheer like mad when he passes successfully to a teammate for a Packer touchdown. "But when the football season is over," says neighbor Mrs. Martha Williamson, "he's just Mr. Starr to the kids."

On occasion, Bart will invite his son and his friends for a ride to the local MacDonald's, where he encourages the boys to stow away all the burgers and milk shakes they can eat.

Other evenings after the football season is over, Bart may join some of his neighbors on the sidewalk for conversations. "But the talk is seldom football," said Bob Stewart. "We talk about our kids, the city government, the neighborhood, and any problems we might be having."

As an active member of the First Methodist Church, and a member of the church's governing board, Bart has been one of the most influential members of the church and is one of the prime reasons that the church is one of the most community-minded organizations in the city of Green Bay.

"He really is one of the finest Christian gentlemen I have ever known," said the Reverend Roger Bourland, pastor of the church. "He is humble, but at the same time dynamic and exciting. One of his greatest characteristics is that he does so much for people in a personal way with his time, talent, and money. And most of them don't know he is responsible.

"He has been very influential in bringing many of the members of the Packers to church services. And Bart, Bill Curry, and Carroll Dale have been providing devotions for the Protestant members of the team, when they are on the road."

At a meeting of the local Cub Scouts, Bart spoke about the kinds of things in life that are important to him, to his family, and to the Green Bay Packers.

"Always play to win," said Bart. "Winning may not be everything, but the effort put forth to win is everything.

"Any game played is worth striving to win. Winning often demands sacrifice. If not, the game wasn't too important.

"Winning requires teamwork. And winning teamwork,

11. Jim Taylor (31), about to get a hand-off from Starr in the 1966 title game. (*Vernon J. Biever Photo*)

12. Starr (15) has just given the ball to Taylor on a reverse. (*Vernon J. Biever Photo*)

13. The Packers would not have had so much success without those Paul Hornung touchdowns. (*Vernon J. Biever Photo*)

14. A dream come true. Commissioner Pete Rozelle presents the Super Bowl Trophy to Coach Lombardi. (*Vernon J. Biever Photo*)

15. Vince and Bart. (*Vernon J. Biever Photo*)

16. A moment of silence in memory of Vincent Thomas Lombardi, 1913–70. (*John E. Biever Photo*)

of course, requires that each member perform his individual assignment to the very best of his ability.

"The winning effort, winning teamwork, a winning performance—they all require proper instructions. Listen, learn and follow instructions. Only then can you turn in the winning performance."

CHAPTER 19

Nineteen sixty-five provided the football world with one of its greatest seasons ever, according to the football historians, and there isn't a football fan in the world who would disagree with them. For sheer excitement and gridiron drama it might be equaled but never surpassed. Through fourteen games the titan elevens of the Western Conference of the National Football League clashed in a magnificent struggle in one of the tightest races in football history for a divisional crown, a race that was not to be decided until a full week after the season's regulation schedule had come to its hectic end. It was a year, too, in which Vince Lombardi's mighty Green Bay Packers were once more to prove, though not without a bitter battle, their dominance in the arenas of the football wars.

In the 1965 Packer training camp, Lombardi, still smarting from his second-place finishes in 1963 and 1964, issued his historic ultimatum.

"This year we are going to be Number One!" he announced to his assembled squad of gridders. "If you don't think we're Number One, I don't want you playing for me! If you can't go out there and win, pack your gear and go home!"

Nobody packed his gear. Nobody went home. Not on his own volition anyway.

Lombardi, as he always did, began to reassess his forces for the coming wars of the 1965 season. First, there was the evaluation of his 1964 squad. Bart Starr had been the leading quarterback of the year and without a doubt was the key to a successful season. He had gradually developed under Lombardi to a point where he was recognized as one of the shrewdest play-callers in pro football. Jim Taylor, Paul Hornung, Tom Moore, and Elijah Pitts had given the Packers the strongest running backs in the league. Willie Davis, Henry Jordon, Ray Nitschke, Herb Adderly, and Willie Wood had developed their skills to a point where they were recognized as the strongest, toughest defense in pro football.

Paul Hornung had lost most of his great kicking abilities; he had booted only 12 of 38 field-goal attempts; and this great weakness had spelled the difference between first place and second. Lombardi's big job was to get a player who could be relied on for those game-winning field goals.

Don Chandler had been an outstanding kicking star for coach Allie Sherman's New York Giants since 1956. But he was weary and tired of shuttling back and forth from New York to his family on the Coast. He wanted to be closer to them and to his other business interests. Lombardi talked to Chandler, persuaded him to play for Green Bay and negotiated this important trade with Coach Sherman.

There were other important additions Lombardi made. He traded for Carroll Dale, a marvelous receiver from the Los Angeles Rams. He picked Georgia Tech's Bill Curry, a fine center, and Junior Coffey, a hard-running back from Washington State.

Nineteen sixty-five was going to be a great year for the Green Bay Packers. It was going to be a magnificent year for Bart Starr. But it wasn't going to be an easy road to the championship. There were a few rude shocks and no little pain, particularly for Bart Starr in that most dramatic of football seasons.

It all started off well enough, for both Starr and his teammates, with a romp over the Pittsburgh Steelers, 41–9. As a matter of fact, Green Bay would go undefeated through the first six games on its schedule. But Bart Starr was to suffer a continuous stream of injuries, injuries that conceivably could shorten his brilliant career.

The second game of the season, Green Bay and the Baltimore Colts met head to head, shoulder to shoulder, almost fist to fist. It was a bruising sixty minutes with neither team giving or asking for quarter. The Packers knew they had to beat Baltimore if they were going to be in the championship race.

It was 10–10 in the third quarter of the game when Bart stepped back into the pocket, quickly scanned the field for his potential receiver, Carroll Dale. He never found him. Ordell Braase, the tough Baltimore right end, smashed through the Packer defense and bowled him over. For a moment both men lay on the ground.

Then Braase got up, calmly glanced at Starr, and walked away.

Bart lay on the ground. His left leg was turned under him. He pawed the ground for a moment, as if to try to get up, then lay still. He was hurt, badly hurt. His teammates had to help him to the side lines.

Fortunately for Green Bay, Zeke Bratkowski was always ready; Zeke, Bart's pal and diligent backup man. Zeke called the signals the way Bart would have called them.

"I pattern my thinking, call the same plays that Bart would," said Zeke. "After the way we've worked together, I think just like he does."

Zeke's fine play was good enough to lead Green Bay to its second victory of the season, 20–17.

The Packers walloped the Bears and the Forty-niners to make it four straight.

The next game with Detroit found Starr ready for the Lions. The Lions were tough. Green Bay couldn't penetrate their defense throughout the whole first half of the game, while the tough Detroit offense battered the Packers for 3 solid touchdowns. At the half, the score was Lions, 21; Green Bay, 3.

"They outplayed us badly," said Bart, summing up that game against Detroit, "but this is a game of pride. In the first half of the game our pride was hurt. A man has to have pride in what he's doing—win, lose, or draw."

Pride, or the return of Bart Starr's pinpoint passing, the story was a bit different in that encounter with the Detroit Lions.

A 62-yard pass, Starr to Bob Long, the Green Bay sophomore end out of Wichita, and the Packers had their first TD of the third quarter, and the game. A few minutes later Starr hit halfback Tom Moore with a 32-yard pass and the play put another Green Bay touchdown on the scoreboard. Another pass, still in the third period, a short one to rookie Carroll Dale and the sensational Dale was off on a 77-yard sprint for the third TD Bart Starr passed of the period.

It was Bart Starr's clever strategy that had made that touchdown possible. It was third down and 2 to go on the Green Bay 23. The Lions' defense felt sure that Starr would hand-off to his big crunching back Jim Taylor for a punch at the line. But Bart faked to Taylor and shot a perfect pass to Dale, who ran the ball all the way in for a score.

Bart himself scored the last touchdown of the afternoon for the Packers, on a 4-yard run sprint around end. Green Bay had won its fifth game in a row.

The Baltimore Colts, however, were keeping pace with the Packers, only one game behind the Conference-leading Green Bay.

The next week, the Packers took the Dallas Cowboys handily, 13–3. The Colts won, too.

Then came the trip to Chicago, a rude halt in the Green Bay drive and near disaster for its star quarterback.

The Bears, out to avenge two straight defeats at the hands of the Packers, were ferocious in their attack and even more ferocious in their defense.

Bart Starr had faded back to pass. He looked for his

receivers. All his receivers were covered. Suddenly Bart spotted an opening in the line, faked a pass and then put his head down and plunged for the opening. He drove ahead for 10 yards and a first down. But he kept on running, twisting, dodging, turning, as he moved up the field for 25 yards, and then he was hit. Roosevelt Taylor, the veteran Bear, slammed into the quarterback, and Bart was down. He was down hard.

Quickly, Vince Lombardi pulled him out of the game and sent in Zeke Bratkowski. The Packers, at this moment in the first quarter, were leading, 7-3.

Bart should have remained out of the rest of the game. But, in a few minutes, he was back again, calling the signals.

"How do you feel?" Vince Lombardi had asked him.

"I'm O.K.," Bart had said.

He wasn't. He was dizzy and weak from the tackle. His timing was off. He called the wrong plays at the wrong time. The Bears walloped the Packers, 31-10, that afternoon, and the Green Bay winning streak was stopped. Baltimore was tied with the Packers for the Western Conference lead.

"I should have taken Bart out and kept him out," said Lombardi after that loss to the Bears. "I thought he was O.K., but I was wrong."

The injury seemed to hang on and bother Bart in the next game against Detroit, a vital one. He was not up to his usual form. His passing was erratic and he was stopped cold several times as the Green Bay attack stuttered and stalled and the Lions, attacking viciously, beat the Packers 12-7.

It was the accurate kicking of Don Chandler, who with just 37 seconds to go, booted his seventh field goal of the season in a fierce battle against the Los Angeles Rams. It gave the Packers the game, 6–3.

Bart Starr was his old self—sharp and accurate—against the Minnesota Vikings. He threw 3 touchdown passes as the Packers romped to a 38–13 victory. But the Baltimore Colts kept right on winning. Green Bay was still one full game behind.

An unexpected loss to the Los Angeles Rams, a second victory over the Vikings, and the Packers' record, after twelve games of the 1965 season, was 9 wins, 3 losses. The Baltimore Colts led the Conference with a 9-2-1 record, and the Chicago Bears were just one game behind Green Bay with 8 wins against 4 losses. With the Packers to meet the Colts in their second meeting of the year, the Conference title was still up for grabs.

Green Bay traveled to Baltimore for the game, giving the Colts the home-team advantage. It didn't help them. Bart Starr was in top form for the game and his game was brilliant. Lou Michaels kicked a field goal for Baltimore at the 4½-minute mark, but the rest of the first quarter belonged to the Packers.

Bart mixed his plays beautifully, sending his backs through the line time after time, then passing the ball when the Colts expected a running attack. He marched his men to the Colt 2-yard line, where Paul Hornung plunged over for the TD. Minutes later Starr hit Paul Hornung with a beautiful 35-yard pass, and Paul smashed into the end zone for Green Bay's second TD of the quarter. In the second quarter he hit Dowler from the 10, and the Packers had their third touchdown of the day.

There was no stopping the Packers with Bart Starr at the helm. In the third quarter Bart marched Green Bay down the field to the 9, where Hornung scored once more; and then to the 3 for an easy plunge for the Golden Boy and his fourth touchdown of the afternoon.

To cap his magnificent performance, in the fourth period Bart passed to Hornung from the Packer 35-yard line, and the Golden Boy went over for his fifth TD of the day.

Baltimore fought valiantly, furiously, but Bart, with 10 completions out of 17 passes, was unbeatable this day, and with Hornung once more at his best, the Packers could not be stopped. Green Bay romped to a 42–27 victory and, with just one game left in the 1965 pro-football schedule, the lead in the dramatic struggle for the 1965 Western Conference championship.

"A victory by Green Bay next Sunday over the San Francisco Forty-niners," wrote the sportswriters, analyzing all the possibilities in the battle for the Conference crown, "would give the Packers the title."

"The Bears," they wrote, "cannot yet be counted out. They're only one game behind the leading Packers, and a Green Bay loss, a Baltimore loss, a Chicago win on the last day of the season, and Chicago would cop the crown."

As for the Colts, they wrote, "A Green Bay loss and a Baltimore win, and the Colts would have it all."

And that's what almost happened.

Baltimore won its game that last Sunday of the regulation pro-football schedule, eliminating the Bears from the race. The Packers didn't do as well. It may have been the result of a let-down after the tremendous victory over the Colts and the knowledge that they were in first place. It may have been overconfidence, and overconfidence has a way of proving fatal. Whatever it was, Bart Starr tossed a 42-yard pass to Boyd Dowler for a TD and engineered the Packers down the field for three more scores that afternoon. It wasn't enough. The Forty-niners, playing inspired football, were the spoilers. They held Green Bay and, in the last seconds of the game, brilliant John Brodie of the Forty-niners zipped a 27-yard pass to rookie Vern Burke in the Packers' end zone, and San Francisco had played the Conference leaders to a 24–24 tie.

The race for the championship of the Western Conference was deadlocked. The Packers and the Colts were to meet once more, for the third time in the 1965 season, and this time the winners would go on, champs of the Western Conference, to meet the Cleveland Browns, champions of the Eastern Conference, for the championship of the world.

That playoff game, in Green Bay on December 26, 1965, was to prove to be one of those games the fans and the sportswriters call "a game for the books." It was a game in which both teams, literally, limped off the field. It was a game in which Bill Anderson, the Packer rookie end from Tennessee, would walk into the clubhouse in a daze, with no memory of the last minutes of the game, with no memory of a crucial pass he had made in the final Packer drive. And he was not the only gridder who left the field in that fuzzy condition.

With the opening gun, the crowd that jammed the Packer stands let out a mighty roar, a roar that would not stop until the last play of the game, leaving the fans hoarse, limp, and almost as exhausted as the gridders. But it was a sudden hush and a cry of despair that came from the stands on the very first play from scrimmage in that momentous battle for the Conference crown.

Green Bay won the toss and elected to receive. The Colts kicked off and the Packers found themselves with the ball on their own 15. Bart Starr looked over the defense, barked out his signals.

"Hut . . . hut, hut!"

He took the snap from center, faked to Jim Taylor, stepped into the pocket and threw a short flat pass to the side lines. It was the kind of play that almost always guarantees 10 yards and a first down.

Bill Anderson was waiting for the pass, had it; but the Colts were on him.

Lenny Lyles, the Baltimore cornerback, hit him hard, and the ball popped out of Anderson's hands.

Don Shinnick, the Colt linebacker, picked it up and headed for the Green Bay end zone, 25 yards away.

There was only one Packer who stood between the runner and a Baltimore touchdown—Bart Starr.

Bart tore after the man with the ball. There was only one way he knew how to play the game—all out. He went after Shinnick. It was his job to stop the run, prevent the touchdown. But he never got to the Colt linebacker. Jim Welch was there to block for the linebacker and, brutally, he bowled over the star Packer quarterback, and Shinnick scored.

Bart lay still on the ground for a moment. That's when a great moan filled the stands. He got up slowly, wracked in pain. His chest and his rib cage were badly bruised. The first play from scrimmage in that all-important game was the last for Bart Starr. He would watch the game from the bench and come on to the field again only to hold the ball when Don Chandler was to attempt a placement kick.

Without Bart, the Packers were without the key man of their club, their brilliant quarterback. They walked into their dressing room at the half with the Colts leading by the score of 10–0.

In the third quarter of the game, Paul Hornung punched over the 1-yard line to give the Pack its first score of the game. With Starr holding, Don Chandler, that most valuable addition to the Green Bay club in 1965, booted the ball for the extra point. It was now Colts, 10; Packers, 7.

It was determined defense on the part of both teams that would not permit another touchdown throughout the remainder of the struggle. But, in the last 2 minutes of the battle, Bart Starr made one more appearance on the gridiron, and held the ball for a Don Chandler boot, and a field goal that tied the game.

That's the way it was as the gun went off to signal the end of sixty minutes of regulation play. The playoff now demanded an extra period—the period that is called "sudden death." The championship of the Conference would now go to the team that scored first.

For 13 minutes of that "sudden death" overtime, the gladiators of the gridiron struggled up and down the field. In the tenth minute the Colts had a chance to put the game away, but the pass from center had been wobbly and Lou Michaels' attempted field goal from the Green Bay 47, missed.

There were less than 2 minutes left to that dramatic overtime, with the prospects of the game requiring still another overtime, when once more and for the last time of the afternoon, Bart Starr made his appearance on the gridiron.

The ball was on the Colt 25. The snap came back from center. Bart placed the ball and Chandler kicked.

The roar from the jam-packed stands was deafening, a dinning crescendo, as Chandler's kick sailed straight and true between the goal posts. It was a roar that was probably heard in every county in Wisconsin as the Green Bay Packers limped off the field, victors in that most dramatic finish to a most dramatic game in a most dramatic season, by the score of 13–10; and champions of the Western Conference once more.

The game for the championship of the National Football League between the Packers and the Cleveland Browns, winners of the Eastern crown, played in Green Bay, on January 2, 1966, was something of an anticlimax.

Three inches of snow fell on Lambeau Field in Green Bay the morning of the championship game. The snow turned to rain, then to sleet. Bart Starr, who was in there despite his aching chest and rib cage, played a heady game. His strategy called for ball control and he kept the game, for the most part, on the ground. He threw a pass to Carroll Dale, after the Packers had received the opening kickoff, and the pass was good enough for 47 yards and the first Green Bay touchdown. After that, he passed infrequently, relying for the most part on his running backs.

Cleveland kept the game very close in the first half, holding the Packers to a 13–12 lead. But the Green Bay line held the Brown's great running back, Jimmy Brown, to a scant 50 yards for the afternoon, held the Eastern Conference champions scoreless in the second half, and sloshed through the mud to their clubhouse and a 23–12 win, and for the third time, under the magnificent coach Vincent Lombardi, the champions of the football world.

For Bart Starr, the 1965 season had provided more aches and pains and injuries than he had ever experienced on the gridiron before. Still, it had been one of his most brilliant years in pro football. Once more he had hit on 50 per cent of his passes, this year 55.8 per cent. He had passed for 2,055 yards and 16 touchdowns. Wisconsin voted him the Wisconsin Athlete of the Year at the end of that hectic season. The honors for Bart Starr, his long-deserved recognition, however, were waiting for him in 1966.

CHAPTER 20

The sportswriters were crowding a small area around Bart Starr in the locker room, shouting above the whooping and hollering in the dressing room. They had just been witness to a most magnificent performance on the gridiron. They wanted the quarterback's story.

"Did you stick to your game plan?"

"Did Dallas make you change your style?"

"How come you took so many gambles? You're supposed to be the conservative quarterback?"

There was no doubt about who was the hero of the game, and the writers were all interviewing Bart for their columns.

Bart Starr, slumped and tired, sat on a stool, sweat and grass stains streaking his face. He looked up at the crush of newspapermen.

"You can't talk in terms of individual performance," he said. "In this game you have to talk in terms of a team. This is the greatest win I've ever had. Everything was so hard all season long. The games against the Colts and the Bears, the playoff against the Colts. Everything."

"You were great out there today!"

"Fantastic!"

"You were the game!" exploded one particularly enthusiastic reporter.

Bart Starr didn't budge from his original and almost humble statement.

"I don't care what you say," he said, "or write; you can't win a football game without forty people. I've got a helluva fine football team behind me. The protection," he added, always finding praise in himself for his teammates, "was outstanding."

Paul Hornung pushed through the crowd of writers, put his arms around the quarterback.

"I've never seen you better," he said to his teammate.

Bart pushed back the smile from his face and barely mumbled, "Thank you."

Then he looked around the room of yelling, happy champions. "This is the only place to be," he said with a tired smile. "This is it—to be with the winners."

Nineteen sixty-six saw a year of momentous changes in the structure of the gridiron world. On June 8, following a series of meetings between the National Football League and the American Football League, an announcement that in 1970 both leagues would merge made for headlines in every major newspaper. The two leagues also jointly announced that at the end of the 1966 season the champions of the NFL would meet the champions of the AFL for the championship of the world in what was to be called the Super Bowl.

The veteran players of the National Football League

were not particularly elated with the announcement. With some justification they considered themselves considerably superior to the American Football League, a justification which was not to last for very long. The AFL gridders, of course, were gratified with the recognition they had finally won, and the fans were delighted with the prospects of still another big gridiron game, the game that would establish without question the football championship of the world.

Vince Lombardi, delighted with the new Super Bowl championship, knew better than anyone else that the playing days of his two great running backs, Jim Taylor and Paul Hornung, were limited, and that the Packers would have to dig down deep to find replacements for his two super stars.

Vince found them in the person of Jim Grabowski out of the University of Illinois. Jim had been a tremendous star at Illinois, topping the scoring records set by Red Grange, the great star of the 1930s. Vince also acquired Donny Anderson, a pile-driving All-American fullback from Texas Tech.

The Packers went right after the Western Conference Championship from the opening game of the season. They walloped their closest rivals of the past year, the Baltimore Colts, 24–3.

In the second game of the '66 season, the Packers traveled to Cleveland to meet the 1965 Eastern Conference champions. The Browns were eager to get some revenge for their defeat in the title game of '65. They almost got their revenge.

Green Bay was on its own 19-yard line. The Browns

were leading by the score of 20–14, and there were only 2½ minutes left in the game.

Bart Starr barked out his signals.

"Hut . . . hut . . . hut, hut!"

A pass to Boyd Dowler, a pass to Marv Fleming, a pass to Donny Anderson, and Bart Starr had the Packers moving. But so was the clock. Third down and Bart took the ball himself for a quarterback sneak and first down.

Seconds to go. Bart took the snap from center, faked a quick pass, stepped back, protected by his blockers, spotted Jim Taylor in the end zone, and whipped a short pass straight and true into Taylor's arms for a Green Bay score.

Don Chandler came in to boot the extra point, and the Packers loped off the field with a 21–20 victory.

That's the way it would go with Green Bay throughout the season. Bart Starr was enjoying one of the greatest seasons in his fabled ten-year career. He completed 156 of his 251 passes that season, for an almost unbelievable 62.2 per cent, 14 times for touchdowns. He was intercepted only 3 times in 14 games, just about once in every hundred times he threw the ball.

With Starr, Kramer, Nitschke, Anderson, Chandler, Dale playing, the Packers romped through their schedule, winning 12, losing 2.

Aching ribs, sore chest notwithstanding, Bart was in there all the way. Only once in that season did he ask Lombardi to pull him out of the game. That was in the second half of their second meeting with the Baltimore

Colts. The pain in his ribs was sharp. It became difficult to lift his arm, throw the ball.

"After a while it got so bad that I couldn't raise my elbow," said Bart. "I just couldn't do it any more."

"He didn't tell me a thing about it," said Vince Lombardi, speaking of his quarterback's performance under the extraordinary pain he was suffering. "He didn't say a thing until he came out."

That's the kind of determination and pride Bart Starr had always displayed, but now he was thirty-two years old, a ten-year veteran and was just now reaching the very peak of his game. It was a year in which he marched the Packers down the field to their fifth Western Conference championship in seven years.

The game for the National Football League title and the right to meet the American Football League champions in the first gridiron Super Bowl was to be played in Dallas. The Cowboys, led by their cool and football-wise coach, Tom Landry, had won the Eastern Conference crown handily. Landry fielded a tough, determined team of players. Don Meredith had earned the right to be compared with the best quarterbacks on the gridiron. He boasted two sterling backs in Don Perkins and Dan Reeves. The ends, Mel Renfro and Pettis Norman, were among the top-ranked receivers in the game. And he had Bob Hayes, one of the fastest men in the world in the 100-yard dash, and certainly the fastest man in football. In addition, Tom Landry could boast that Dallas had one of the toughest defenses in the league, led by such stalwarts as Jethro Pugh and Willie Townes.

The battle for the championship of the National

Football League crown in 1966 promised to be a cliff-hanger, and it was.

"If Bart Starr has a good day," said Vince Lombardi, "we'll win. If Don Meredith has a good day," he added, "Dallas will take it."

Don Meredith would have a great day. Bart Starr's day would be nothing less than brilliant.

The Packers started with a rush in that great battle for the league crown. Early in the first quarter, Bart found Elijah Pitts in the end zone and whipped a 17-yard pass into the arms of his receiver for a Packer TD. Chandler converted.

Moments later, rookie Jim Grabowski picked up a Dallas fumble and raced 19 yards for the Green Bay second score. Again Chandler converted, and it was Packers, 14; Cowboys, 0.

For the moment it looked like a Green Bay rout. But the 76,000 screaming Cowboys fans, rocking the Dallas stadium, knew the game was far from over. So did the Packers. The Cowboys were an explosive team, and they could score at any moment.

Don Meredith, undaunted by the Packers' two quick TD's, took command. He sent his big backs, Don Perkins and Dan Reeves into the vaunted Green Bay line for long yardage, and before the first quarter was over, Reeves and Perkins had each smashed their way into the Packers' end zone, Danny Villanueva converted twice, and the score was Packers, 14; Cowboys, 14, as the period ended.

In the second period, Starr connected with his second touchdown pass of the game, a 51-yard bomb to Carroll

Dale. A third Don Chandler conversion made it Green Bay, 21; Dallas, 14.

The Packer line stiffened. Don Meredith kept his men moving but all they could get in the rest of the first half of that bruising game was a field goal by Danny Villanueva. Green Bay went into its locker room, between halves, with a 4-point margin. A 4-point lead means very little in a pro gridiron game; it would mean less in this championship game, as Green Bay would soon get to know.

Dallas opened the scoring in the third period with a second Villanueva field goal and the Cowboys now trailed the Packers by just 1 point. Before the end of that period, however, Bart Starr once more found his receiver waiting for a pass, and he zipped one down to young Boyd Dowler, for Bart's third touchdown pass of the game. Chandler converted. Score: Green Bay, 28; Dallas, 20.

With less than 5 minutes to play, Starr once again hurled a pass that was good for a Packer touchdown. This one to veteran Max McGee for 26 yards and the TD. Chandler, for once, failed to convert, but Green Bay was leading by a comfortable 34–20. The game was almost won, and the championship with it, or so it seemed to both the Packers and the 76,000 silent fans in the stands.

Normally the talk would have been all about Bart Starr's brilliant performance, his 4 touchdown passes, but Don Meredith had other ideas and, in a matter of moments, the silence in the stands turned into a mighty roar.

With just 4 minutes left on the game clock, Meredith hurled a 68-yard pass for a touchdown to his tight end, Frank Clarke. Villanueva converted and, abruptly, the Cowboys trailed by just 7 points, a touchdown and conversion.

The Packers tried to kill the clock. They couldn't. Dallas took control of the ball again, and 2½ minutes in which to tie the game and send it into an extra period and sudden-death.

"Go! Go! Go!" screamed the fans, and Meredith replied.

He drove the Cowboys over the mid-stripe, to the Packers' 47.

"Go! Go!"

Meredith took the ball from center, then made a quick toss to Frank Clarke. The Cowboys were on the Packers' 26!

"Go . . . !"

Again Dandy Don hit Clarke. The Packers' safety saved the TD, dragging Clarke down on the 2-yard line.

One minute and fifty-two seconds may prove a lifetime in football. One minute and fifty-two seconds and the Cowboys with first down on the Green Bay 2, and the sudden-death period seemed a certainty.

"Go!" yelled the delirious fans.

Dan Reeves hit the Packers' line. The line held, but Reeves was down on the 1.

"Go!" pleaded the fans, hysterically.

Meredith zipped the ball to Norman in the end zone. Norman had it, but lost control and the ball slithered from his eager fingertips. On the next play, the Cowboys had been off side. They were back on the Green Bay 6.

With two downs to make those 6 yards, and the din of the crowds in his ears, Don whipped the ball to Pettis Norman. This time Norman held the ball, on the Packers' 2.

One more chance, one more try, that was all that Meredith had to move his team across the end line, tie the score. Would it be a run? Would it be a pass? Would he send Reeves or Perkins through the stubborn Green Bay defense?

On the field they could barely hear the signals the quarterback barked in his characteristic staccato, for the din of the fans in the stadium.

The ball was snapped from center. It was an option play that Meredith had called. He moved to his right and the Packers' defensive back, Dave Robinson moved right in at him. Meredith dropped back. He was on the 10-yard line, his eyes on the end zone, straining to find a receiver.

Everyone, Packer and Cowboy, was in the end zone, and Robinson, in pursuit, his arms up in the air!

Meredith had to throw the ball. A desperation pass! That was all that was left to him! A desperate attempt to reach a receiver in the Packers' end zone.

He threw the pigskin. Bob Hayes, the fastest man on the field, went after it. So did Tom Brown, the Packers' defensive halfback. And it was Tom Brown who won the race, gathered in the ball and went down.

Green Bay had won the title.

It had been a great day for football, a great day for

both the Green Bay Packers and the Dallas Cowboys. It had been one of Bart Starr's greatest days on the gridiron.

"There were at least two plays," wrote a sportswriter, "on which Starr accomplished the impossible. Once when he was hit by the 271-pound Willie Townes around the ankles and still managed to get a 12-yard completion to his back, Jim Taylor.

"Another was when Willie Townes, tackle Jim Colvin, and right linebacker Dave Edwards came at him, at once, in a blitz; and Starr just danced to the right, stepped forward almost to the scrimmage line, and snapped off a brilliant throw to Max McGee at the goal line, for a touchdown."

They counted the number of times Bart had thrown a pass when the Packers were deep in their own territory and asked, "Is this the quarterback who plays a conservative game?"

"He showed a courage," they wrote, "that is born only out of supreme confidence."

Benny Friedman, who had been one of the truly great quarterbacks when he played the game for the Chicago Bears in the 1930s said, "Bart Starr adheres to three principles with almost religious fervor:

"He sizes up the defense with an eye to Barnum's rule that 'there's a sucker born every minute.'

"He disdains the bomb as a weapon of a madman, who may very well blow himself up, to concentrate on short-range, pin-point passing.

"He plays for lateral position so as never to be caught penned up at the hash mark against the sidelines."

17. Bart is never too busy to have a chat with his Green Bay neighbors.

18. And youth groups get a lot of his time.

19. Starr, the new coach, addresses his Green Bay team.
(*Roger Wentowski Photo*)

20. Bart Starr at home in his office. (*Vernon J. Biever Photo*)

It was these principles which Bart Starr carried with him into the first Super Bowl to be played in pro football. The game took place on January 15, in the huge Memorial Stadium in Los Angeles. Ninety-three thousand fans in the stadium and countless millions on TV (there wasn't a soul on the streets of Green Bay) watched the master at work, as he picked the defenses of Hank Stram's Kansas City Chiefs to pieces.

The American Football League champions were no match for the cool brilliance of the Packers' quarterback. He threw 2 touchdown passes to aging Max McGee, one from the 37-yard line, another from the 13. Starr would have had a third TD pass, this one to Carroll Dale, if the play hadn't been nullified by a penalty. For the rest, he ran his men through the Kansas City line or threw those 10- and 15-yard bread-and-butter passes for which he was famous till the game was solidly on ice, after which his pal, Zeke Bratkowski, came in, along with most of Green Bays' second stringers, just for the sport of having played in the Bowl.

The Super Bowl was an anticlimax to a great season, the Packers taking it 35–10, but it gave Green Bay the undisputed title to the world football crown. As for their great quarterback, this was the year when he was finally to receive the honors long due him.

It was Bart Starr who was voted the Most Valuable Player in the game for the title of the football world, in the Los Angeles Memorial Stadium.

Then, at long last recognizing Starr for the great gridder he was, the sportswriter balloting in the United

Press International named the magnificent quarterback the National Football League Player of the Year.

Don Meredith, safety-man Larry Wilson of the St. Louis Cardinals, fullback Leroy Kelly of the Cleveland Browns, each received four of the sportswriters' votes, and tied for the runner-up position in the balloting. Bart Starr ran away from the field, collecting twenty-three of the votes, in an overwhelming endorsement of his mastery of the game.

"Bart Starr is a master tactician," wrote the sportswriters.

He was more than that. He was a great football player. Certainly, in 1966 he was the greatest.

This was the year when Bart Starr was the first recipient of the Byron White Award, the National Football League award for citizenship given to the person who best displays the qualities of a true professional athlete.

CHAPTER 21

Nineteen sixty-seven was another year of broad change in the football world. The National Football League was expanded to include sixteen clubs. The sixteen clubs were divided into four divisions: Century, Capitol, Central, and Coastal. There were to be two playoff games for the NFL championship, instead of one, the title-holder to meet the champions of the American Football League again in a Super Bowl match.

There were changes, too, for the Green Bay Packers. They had to give up the Golden Boy, Paul Hornung, to one of the expansion teams, the New Orleans Saints. Jim Taylor, the all-pro back, played out his option in 1966, and joined the Saints on his own. Vincent Lombardi still had Elijah Pitts, but the Gold Dust Twins—Donny Anderson and Jim Grabowski—had yet to prove themselves on the gridiron. Vince managed to trade for Chuck Mercein, a great star at Yale, then for the New York Giants and the Washington Redskins. It was to be one of the most advantageous deals Lombardi ever made.

He also picked up flashy Travis Williams, the star

back from Arizona State and one of the fastest men in football, and Don Horn, San Diego State's brilliant quarterback. But everybody knew that the fortunes of the Green Bay Packers would ride with the performance of Bart Starr; that their achievement of an incredible record of three consecutive world championships depended on their 1966 Player of the Year.

The beginning of the 1967 football year was something less than a happy one for Bart Starr, who had been voted the 1966 National Football League's Most Valuable Player. In an early preseason exhibition game the thumb of his throwing hand was badly injured. In another preseason game, against the Chicago Bears, his ribs were badly hurt again. He had to sit out two other exhibition games, against the Dallas Cowboys and the Cleveland Browns. It was an injured and hurting Bart Starr who threw for 9 interceptions in the first 2 regulation games of the season. The season before, he had been intercepted only 3 times in 14 games.

In the first regular game of the season, the Detroit Lions intercepted 4 of Bart's passes and were leading the Packers, 17–0, at the half. The Packers, tongue-lashed by Lombardi in the locker room, tore out for the second half of the game and scored 2 quick touchdowns. Then with but a few minutes to play, Don Chandler booted a field goal to tie the score at 17–17 as the game ended.

"We were lucky to tie," said Lombardi, in an ugly mood. "This is no way to kickoff a championship season!"

The Packers took their second game, but once again it

took a last-minute, 46-yard field goal by Chandler to beat their next-door rivals, the Chicago Bears, 13–10.

Coach Lombardi didn't chew out his team this time. "Every game, this year, is going to be a tough one," he said. "Every team is pointing for us and trying to beat us. It's going to be a rough, tough battle all the way, but if we stay healthy, we're going to win!"

In its third game, against the Atlanta Falcons, the Packers blasted through to a 23–0 victory, but the win was a costly one. In the very first quarter, Atlanta's Bob Riggle blitzed through, banged into Starr, as Bart got set to pass. Tommy Nobis, the Atlanta linebacker, drove through and also hit Starr full force. Knocked to the ground, Bart got to his feet slowly. He had been hit hard by Nobis and had taken the force of the charge on his right side, under his previously injured rib cage. He could feel his right arm grow numb. He slowly walked off the field, holding his injured side. He was through for the day. It was going to be some time before he could play with his old-time skill for the Packers. Zeke Bratkowski took over for Bart and guided the team to victory.

The Packers would beat the Lions in their next encounter, then lose to the Minnesota Vikings. They would beat the Cardinals and the Giants, then lose to the Colts. It was an unhappy Vince Lombardi who snapped, when the reporters asked him when Bart Starr would play again.

"How should I know! He could be ready now. He could be ready in a week!"

When Bart was asked when he would be back in the line-up he was more quiet, more civil.

"I'm sorry," he said, "but I don't have anything to say. I'm not trying to be rude," he added in his characteristic style. "I just don't have anything to say."

Pressured by the sportswriters, Bart informed them that he had been to see the doctor, "but the doctor was out."

The writers had to know more.

"What about your arm?"

"It's sore," said Bart. "That's all it is. Just sore."

One bit of fortune for the Green Bay Packers that season was that the other three clubs in the Central Division of the National Football League were for that year, relatively weak. The Packers' 9-4-1 record was enough to give them their Divisional crown. They were even more fortunate, however, in that Bart Starr, who had been in and out of the line-up for most of the season, and hurting badly, was in the best condition of the year and fit for the championship game.

The Los Angeles Rams, the team the Packers were to meet in the inter-Division game, had had a terrific season. They had the best won-and-lost record in National League ball. They had won 11, tied 2, and lost only once. They were the odds-on favorites to whip Vince Lombardi's Green Bay "old men," as they were now being called, with or without Bart Starr.

"We've heard the 'old men' talk before," said Vince Lombardi. There was a gleam in his eye and thunder in his voice as he spoke to his team.

"We're wounded," said Lombardi. "We're hurting.

The sportswriters are picking the Rams, but they'd better be ready to play the game of their lives when they come into Milwaukee. We're going to beat the daylights out of them!

"The Rams are good," continued Lombardi. "They're on a hot winning streak. But they can be beaten. It's going to take an all-out team effort, but we can beat them. And we will!"

Bart Starr led his Packers as the big game opened, and quickly established the fact that he was in top form as he moved the Green Bay offense deep into the Rams' territory, but a Green Bay fumble stalled their offense and Roman Gabriel, the fine Los Angeles quarterback, took over and quickly passed for a Ram TD. An intercepted pass and the Rams were on the Green Bay 10-yard line, apparently on the way to another score.

But the Packer line held. Dave Robinson broke through the Rams' defense and blocked a field-goal attempt, and from there on in, it was all Green Bay.

Travis Williams took a short pass from Starr, broke through the Los Angeles line, and sprinted through the entire L.A. defense for 46 yards and a Green Bay touchdown. Bart Starr was brilliant as he took command and called one of his finest games. He noticed a weak spot in the L.A. defense, sent Carroll Dale into the area and zipped a pass to Carroll for another touchdown. At the half it was Green Bay, 14; Los Angeles, 7.

At the start of the second half Starr tossed 2 more passes that brought the Packers down to the Rams' 6-yard line. Then Bart sent Chuck Mercein crashing into the Los Angeles end zone. Travis Williams broke through the Rams' defenses for a fourth Packer TD, and the Green Bay warriors trotted off the field with a 28–7 victory and the championship of the Western Division. Once more, for the second time in two years, the Packers were to meet the Dallas Cowboys for the National Football League crown.

The Cowboys had walloped the Cleveland Browns by the score of 52–14 to take the Eastern Conference title. They were a team bent on vengeance, still smarting from their loss to the Packers in the 1966 championship game. Once again Green Bay was the underdog. At least, that is the way the sportswriters saw it. But once again, the Packers proved the experts could miss the mark and be wrong.

The story of this game, one of the greatest games in football's history, has been told in the first chapter of this book: the seesaw struggle between the two determined teams; the last-minute drive engineered by Bart Starr, with the Cowboys holding a 17–14 lead; the daring play of Starr, in the last seconds of the game, the quarterback sneak and the great Bart Starr carrying the ball over into the Dallas end zone for the winning touchdown, the winning touchdown and the championship of the National Football League—the unprecedented third consecutive NFL championship for the Green Bay Packers. It is a story that has been rewritten countless times and will be written again. It is a story and a chapter in football's history that will not be forgotten.

Super Bowl II was to be played in the Orange Bowl Stadium, Miami, Florida, on January 14, 1968. The

Packers' opponents were the Oakland Raiders who had romped through their 1967 season, winning 13 games and losing only 1. Led by coach John Rauch, they were expected to make it a close game and, according to a good many writers, take the championship away from Green Bay.

The Raiders had a formidable offense. Daryle Lamonica, their quarterback was being compared, favorably, with Bart Starr. Pete Banaszak was an impressive running back. Fred Biletnikoff was a top-notch flanker. Gene Upshaw a rookie lineman had developed into one of the best in football. Jim Otto was an all-star center.

On defense; the Oakland club had two excellent pass-rushers in Tom Keating and Ike Lassiter. They had six-foot-seven, 265-pound defensive right end Ben Davidson, the man they called "an animal, a blood-thirsty savage." Cherry Starr, Bart's wife, tells of the time the mere sight of him had almost frightened her dog to death.

"Our dog is a good watch dog," she says, "and very brave. But one look at Ben and she ran howling, and hid herself under a bed."

The Raiders also had the veteran, George Blanda, to go for those most important field goals and points-after-touchdown.

As for the Packers, it might have been expected that they had left too much behind them in the titanic struggle against the Dallas Cowboys. It might have been expected that there would be some let-down in their game. But, contrary to what many might have expected, Green Bay ran out on to the field to the rousing cheers of the 75,546 fans who jammed the Miami Stadium; and, if their was any let-down in their game, no one—writers, fans, the millions who watched the game on television— could spot it.

The first time the Packers had the ball, Starr moved the team from their own 34 to the Raiders 32, from where Don Chandler kicked a 39-yard field goal for the first score of the game.

As the first quarter drew to a close, Bart drove his team down the field again, this time from the Packers' 3 to the Raiders' 13, where Chandler's kick was good enough for his second field goal of the afternoon and a Green Bay lead of 6–0.

Early in the second quarter, Bart Starr, reading the Raiders' defense perfectly, wound up and tossed a 62-yard bomb, one of the longest of his career, from his own 38-yard line to Boyd Dowler deep in Raider territory, and Dowler sprinted the last 5 yards to the first Packer TD of the game.

Oakland managed a touchdown in the same period, but Bart, moving the Packers with comparative ease, drove to the Raiders' 36, where Don Chandler, with but 6 seconds of the first half of the game, delivered his third field goal. Green Bay led, 16–7, at the half, a 9-point lead.

"Nine points isn't enough," said Lombardi to his squad in the clubhouse between halves.

Early in the third period, Bart gave the fans an exhibition of how great a quarterback he was. Third down and on his own 40-yard line, Bart faked the ball to Donnie Anderson, who kept driving into the line, then passed the ball to Max McGee. Bart had noticed Raider

Rodger Bird coming toward the right side of McGee, and whipped the ball over to McGee's left shoulder and away from Bird. The pass was good for 35 yards.

Short passes to Donny Anderson and Carroll Dale took the pigskin to the Raider 2, from where Donny Anderson plunged over the Oakland end line. The score following another Chandler conversion: Packers, 23; Raiders, 7.

Herb Adderly intercepted a Daryle Lamonica pass and sprinted through the entire Raider defense for a third Packer TD. Don Chandler had one of his greatest days, booting home 4 field goals. Lamonica managed a second score for the Raiders in the fourth quarter, with the game already lost. And that's the way the day ended.

Green Bay had won it again, this time by the score of 33–14. The Packers had won the world championship of football for the third time in a row, an unprecedented feat, and fulfilled the dream of its coach, Vincent Lombardi. Up in the press box, for the second time in a row, the sportswriters voted Bart Starr the outstanding star of the game.

In the winner's locker room, Bart was surrounded by all the men of the press, and again, typically, he refused to be singled out in the Packer victory.

"You cheat yourself and your coach and your organization," he said, "if you put forth anything less than your total capacity for giving. And we all gave what we had."

The man who always addresses older men as "Mr." and still answers questions with a "No, sir," or a "Yes, sir," talking of his teammates in that victory-celebrating clubhouse, found words one doesn't get very often from a star performer, wherever that star performs.

"There is respect and admiration among us," he said. "We're forty guys and all forty of us feel that way. The whole squad. Not eleven. Not twenty-two. Forty."

He hesitates only a moment, then adds, "It may sound a little corny to anyone else. To us it's as genuine as sunshine."

CHAPTER 22

The 1967 season had been a long, difficult one for the Packers, quarterback Bart Starr, and Coach Lombardi. The team had beaten the Rams for the Western Conference title, beaten Dallas for the NFL title in the subfreezing cold, and at this moment was down in Florida finishing up their last practice session before taking on the Oakland Raiders in the second Super Bowl.

Following that last Friday afternoon practice, Lombardi called the team together. "I just want to say, first of all," he began, "that we all know we can win our second Super Bowl on Sunday. But we are all old hands at this game, and we also know we have to work harder than ever without letting up for one minute." The players began searching each other out, questioning each other with "what's-he-trying-to-say?" looks. Then Lombardi continued:

"I want . . . to tell you how very proud I am of . . . all of you." There was a slight catch in his throat and he was far from being the forceful speaker he usually was at these meetings. "I have told you before that you are the finest team in professional football. It's been a long season and Sunday . . . may be the very last time we are all together. Let's make it a great game, one we can all be proud of."

And so Bart Starr and Jerry Kramer and Forrest Gregg and all the Packers immediately understood: the Green Bay-Oakland Super Bowl was to be Lombardi's last game as the Packer coach. All week long, there had been subtle hints, and now they came flooding back to the Packer players—the tone of finality in Lombardi's voice, the extra closeness with the squad, the old Packers coming down for the game from all over the nation, like a reunion. All the rumors, all the questions. And now the players knew for sure.

Vince's wife, Marie Lombardi, had known all season. "He would come home," she said, "during the times that Starr and Kramer were hurt and the team was in a slump, and he'd get in that big chair, and he was so mentally and physically beaten. He'd say, 'What's the matter with the world today? What's the matter with people? I have to go on that field every day and whip people. It's for them, not just me, and I'm getting to be an animal.'"

The Packers went out and played the last one for the coach, whipping Oakland, 33–14. And at the final gun Lombardi embraced Starr and Kramer and everybody he could put his hands on. And then Kramer and Gregg lifted Lombardi on their shoulders. "One more time, Coach," Kramer said. And Lombardi looked down, tears rolling down his cheeks and said, "Without a doubt this is the best way to leave the football field."

Back in Green Bay a week after the game, Lombardi

met with Phil Bengtson and told him that he was moving out of coaching and would handle the general manager's job only. Bengtson was to be named the new coach. It was decided that the official announcement would be made on February 1, at a sports dinner at the Oneida Golf and Riding Club.

Lombardi took nearly two full weeks between the Super Bowl and the day of the announcement to prepare his little five-page speech. When the time came, what had started out as an intimate gathering of friends of the Packers had swelled to more than one hundred people, most of them newsmen. Finally Lombardi stepped to the microphone. "What I have to say," he began, "is not completely without emotion. Because of the emotion involved, I felt I could not trust myself to say what I must say unless it was written down." After talking of the growth of pro football, the growth of the Packers, and the increase of the responsibilities, the audience began to get a little restive. But as Lombardi began his closing, the entire room grew silent. "I believe it is impractical for me to continue to coach and be the general manager, and feel I must relinquish one of them. Gentlemen, let me introduce the new head coach of the Packers, Phil Bengtson."

He turned to Bengtson and Packer president Dom Olejniczak and began to lead the applause for his successor. There were tears cascading down his cheeks as the Lombardi era came to a close.

At the rear of the crowded, noisy club, Bart Starr and Zeke Bratkowski sat in stony silence as Lombardi introduced the new Green Bay coach. The two great quarterbacks sat together with heads bowed, and then suddenly the newsmen surrounded them with questions, and the memories came flooding back to Starr as he brushed away the tears.

"There was a poem that Coach Lombardi recited that I shall never forget," said Bart.

> Out of our beliefs are born deeds.
> Out of our deeds we form habits.
> Out of our habits grow our characters.
> On our character we build our destination.

"These words," said Bart, "represent to me the essence of the man, Vince Lombardi. I cannot say enough about him, but I will try. To me, Vince Lombardi will always be the greatest football coach who ever lived. But there's so much more to it than that. I love Coach Lombardi like I love my own dad, and I don't mind saying so. Everything I am as a man and as a football player I owe to him. He is the man who taught me almost everything I know about football, about leadership, and about life. He took a kid from Montgomery, Alabama, and made a man out of him. With his example, with his leadership, with his faith. Maybe I could have done it myself. Maybe. Coach Lombardi has always refused to take credit for whatever success his players achieved. He has always believed that a man grasps his destiny in his own hands. But I know the debt of gratitude I can never repay.

"The first time I met Coach Lombardi was in June 1959," said Bart. "He was looking forward to his first year as head coach of the Green Bay Packers. I was not exactly looking forward to my third season with the Packers. During my first two seasons, we had losing teams. I did not get to play much, and when I did, I did not play well. That June, Coach Lombardi invited his four quarterbacks and a few receivers to an indoctrination session. The idea was to get a head start on our passing game."

Bart continued, "My first impression of Coach Lombardi is one I never had reason to change. I thought he was the best-organized, most forceful, most dynamic, most influential man I had ever met. It was a strange feeling sitting there and listening to him talk. I was fully aware that my life was being transformed. I wanted to go out and play football for this man right then and there. I couldn't wait.

"Coach Lombardi's desire for excellence burned inside him like a blow torch," said Bart, "and he transmitted that flame to his players. He showed me the meaning and value of mental toughness. He said that when he first met me he had some doubts that I would become a winning quarterback because I was too 'nice.' He was right. I worried too much about the mistakes I *might make*—and about the ones I had made. I was willing to settle for less than absolute control of the team.

"I guess that's how I feel about Coach Lombardi," said Bart, walking out into the darkened sky. He looked up into the stars for a brief moment, then turned to his good friend Zeke Bratkowski saying, "Zeke, it'll never be the same without him."

CHAPTER 23

Bart Starr, crouched over the center, was barking signals for a pass play.

"Thirty-five, twenty-two . . ." yelled Starr.

"Fifty-two . . . Yow!"

Zeke Bratkowski had been tiptoeing up on Starr and all the Packers saw what was happening, and they were trying to stop their laughter.

Zeke had scooped up some muddy water from the playing field, holding it carefully in his palm. Directly in front of him, Starr called out the signals. Suddenly Zeke dropped the cold, muddy water on the back of Bart's neck, and Bart yelled out in surprise and jumped a foot off the ground. The entire Packer squad burst out laughing.

Bart turned, his hand reaching back to wipe the water off. "You son of a gun," Bart laughed, "you really got me by surprise this time."

Zeke shook, he was laughing so hard. Bart turned to a writer on the side lines who had witnessed the play. "Zeke does that all the time," said Bart. "You'd swear someone had sneezed all over you."

The times were indeed changing for the Packers. The Lombardi era had ended, and much of that intangible Lombardi spirit was a thing of the past.

Phil Bengtson, the new head coach, was a fine coach with a brilliant record as an assistant to Vince Lombardi for ten years. He had been an All-American tackle at the University in 1933–34 and had been an assistant coach at Missouri and at Stanford University as well as line coach for the San Francisco Forty-niners. But stepping in as coach of the Green Bay Packers, taking over Vince Lombardi's job, was indeed a monumental task.

It was a frustrating year and an ordeal for Bengtson, and it was a frustrating year for Bart Starr and the rest of the Packers.

Bart injured the little finger on his passing hand during an early season game, pulled a tendon in his bicep muscle, injured and reinjured his rib cage. Consequently, Starr was to miss three entire games of the 1968 season and play only parts of three other games. Jerry Kramer and Carroll Dale came down with injuries, but the biggest blow and the most severe was the loss of Don Chandler, the great kicking specialist of the Packers. Don retired from the game for business reasons, and his loss was a severe blow to the fortunes of the team.

Bart began the 1968 football season with all the dash and vigor and brilliance the fans had grown accustomed to. In September, against the Minnesota Vikings, he completed 14 of 22 passes, one to the star receiver Carroll Dale for a Packer touchdown. Again, in September, against the Detroit Lions, he tossed 2 touchdown passes to Carroll Dale, one a 63-yard bomb. Early in October he again found his receiver for 2 Green Bay TDs.

But in those first five games of the 1968 season the Packers were able to walk off the field with only 2 victories.

Coach Bengtson made absolutely clear the importance of Bart Starr to the Packers.

"I don't want to detract from Zeke Bratkowski," he said, referring to Bart's backup quarterback, "but Starr was the leading factor in our attack. Our game was designed around the things he could do, and we didn't have him available for a good share of the time. That's just a fact."

How important Bart Starr was to his team may be judged from just two isolated items. In his first four games of 1968 he completed close to 65 per cent of his passes. In the game in which he appeared for just one play, against the Lions, late in October, he tossed a forward pass to Dowler that was good for a touchdown and a 14–14 tie with the Detroit Club.

Against the Atlanta Falcons, Bart hurled another 2 touchdown passes, and then was racked up by the Falcon defense. He was out of the game for two weeks.

He was back for that lone play against Detroit. He tossed a 50-yard bomb to Carroll Dale in a losing cause against the Chicago Bears, but led the Packers to a 28–17 win over the Dallas Cowboys with 4 touchdown passes: a 28-yard pass to Dale, a 10-yard pass to Marv Fleming, a 32-yard pass to Fleming again, and a fourth quarter 20-yard pass to Boyd Dowler.

Green Bay wound up the season with a record of 6

wins against 7 losses and a tie. It was their first losing season since 1958.

To make matters worse, much worse, Bart suffered a shoulder separation in the last game of the year, against the Chicago Bears. It was an injury that would lead, in time, to the end of his playing days.

"We have eighty arms on the team," said Coach Bengtson to his star quarterback, "and you have to hurt the only one that counts."

Bart Starr discounted that kind of judgment. He repeated, as he had done so often, "There are forty men in the team. It's all forty who win the game."

But there was something more in Bart's game, something he rarely or ever mentioned.

"I guess the good Lord takes care of you in things like that," he would say.

"The things like that" might refer to a brilliant play on the gridiron, a lucky break, an escape from some crippling injury.

Bart had an abiding faith in the Lord, still has an abiding faith in the Lord, and it has been and is still evident in his works both on and off the playing field.

He has worked and continues to work for any number of charitable organizations. With his wife, Cherry, he ran a telethon to help in a drive to raise funds to battle the dread cerebral palsy. With Cherry he has been state chairman for an Easter Seal campaign. He raised $45,000 for a camp for underprivileged boys by donating the *Sport* Magazine Corvette he won for being named the Most Valuable Player in the 1967–68 Super Bowl. And he was recognized for all his sincere work for his community, his state, and his nation by receiving the National Football League Gladiators Award "for outstanding contribution to community and pro football" in 1969.

"Bart goes to chapel alone each week," says his wife Cherry, "and prays for guidance to be a good leader for his club. Each evening, before going to bed, he reads inspirational material that is based on the Holy Scriptures."

It is scarcely to be wondered that men in the public eye have a great responsibility.

"They are idolized by the young people," says Bart Starr, "and the young people set their patterns according to their heroes."

Bart has in mind his own two young sons, Bart, Jr., and Brett, when he speaks of the image of the professional athlete and the influence of that image on youngsters. He is bothered occasionally by some of the antics, the drunken driving, the all-night gambling, the sprees of a few football players, as they are reported in the press. But more than anyone else, Bart is concerned about his own image and makes certain it is the best kind of image he can present to all around him by adhering to the tenets of his faith and practicing them faithfully. There is nothing pretentious about Bart Starr. Nothing false. He is a natural man and his thinking, speaking, actions are most natural.

When he was asked what makes a good quarterback, he thought for a moment, then spoke simply and directly.

"You have to be dedicated," he said. "I mean that

sincerely. You've got to give it everything you've got, and I can't say that often enough. And you've got to love what you're doing."

Sincerity, simplicity, dedication, and love, Bart Starr gave them all to the game. What is more, he gave of himself, these same inherent qualities, to everybody around him, on the gridiron and off it.

Bart Starr completed 109 passes for 1,617 yards in his limited appearance on the football field in 1968. He threw 15 passes for touchdowns, and his passing average was an incredible 63.7 per cent—the best passing percentage he was to achieve in his entire career. But the fans, watching Starr, knew that the great quarterback had peaked in his performance. The big question was, "How long can he hold this peak?"

The life of an athlete in any of the sports arenas, baseball, boxing, basketball, hockey, track, football, is limited. Wishes and hopes for the continued great performance of the great quarterback were rich in hope and fervor, but the doubts had already begun to set in.

CHAPTER 24

In 1968 Bart Starr had led the National Football League
in pass completions. He was going to lead the league
again, in 1969, with a pass completion average of 62.2
per cent and the fewest interceptions: 6. He would continue to be the nation's leading quarterback, and his pin-
point passing would be as accurate as it always had
been. But the injuries he had suffered during his more
than twelve years on the gridiron, particularly his injuries
during the past season, hampered his play, would cut
into his playing time. He would miss the last four games
of the season completely.

In a slam-bang game against the Detroit Lions, Bart
stepped back to throw a pass, but the Lions, battling the
Packers' defense savagely, broke through and three huge
Lion tacklers smashed into Starr simultaneously. When
he arose, his right arm dangled uselessly at his side, and
he clutched his shoulder as he staggered to the side
lines. The injury, a painful shoulder separation, was to
hamper Bart during the rest of the year.

"I had had a shoulder separation before," said Bart,
"and I just had it taped up properly and never missed a

game, not even a preseason game. But this one is more severe. I can't throw the ball."

The Packers had a fair season in 1969, winning 8 games, losing close, hard-fought battles to the Los Angeles Rams, the Colts, Vikings (twice), Lions, and the Cleveland Browns.

The 8-6 record was good enough for third place, behind the Detroit Lions and the Vikings.

As the season drew to an unhappy finish, Bart Starr set out to improve his physical condition, so that he would be fit for the 1970 season. His arm, shoulder, rib cage had been injured and reinjured, and with the aid and advice of Dominic Gentile, the Green Bay trainer, he developed a rigorous training program for himself.

He began each morning with a six-mile run. Then, in the training room under the Lambeau Field grandstand, he worked on special exercises on the weight machine, lifted barbells, and went through a series of complicated isometric and isotonic exercises. He had installed a wheel with a handle, on one wall of the training room. Its height was adjusted so that one complete turn of the handle extended his arm and his shoulder muscles. Bart worked at that wheel and handle five and ten minutes a day, religiously. He finished off his daily routine by first lobbing a football, then increasing the pressure gradually until he could throw the ball, easily, fluidly, yet with great speed to his receivers.

Day after day Bart went through the grueling routine, until one day late in July he felt he was ready for his fourteenth year of professional football.

"I love the game," he said. "I love to play football

today just as much as I loved to play when I was back in high school."

There had been a moment when he thought of retiring, putting away his cleats and hanging up his uniform, right after Super Bowl II.

"My wife, Cherry, wants me to continue playing as long as I want to play," said Bart. "And a couple of years ago, when I asked Bart, Jr., how he felt about my possibly retiring, he said, 'Gee, Dad, if you quit now, Brett will never get to see you play!'

"We had a thing with both our boys," said Bart, "that they would get to start going to our games when they were six years old. Brett turned six in 1970.

"I thought about retiring when Coach Lombardi stepped down," says Bart, explaining his change of mind, "and I just couldn't walk out on Phil Bengtson."

Not even for a run for a seat in the United States Senate. Back in 1968, the Republican Party had called on Bart. They wanted him to run against William Proxmire, and they figured he could beat the incumbent. But Bart wasn't ready to retire, just yet.

He had campaigned and will campaign in the future for his party but, "I have no political ambitions for myself," he says.

Bart feels that a man can and should be involved in public life, but he has reservations about public office.

"If you're not independently wealthy, you have to ask others to donate to your campaign," he says. "When you do that, you've lost your independence. I can't compromise my principles that way."

Bart Starr may change his mind some day about going

into politics. Things like that happen. But he would never change his mind about, or his attitude toward, his principles. In 1970 the great quarterback was primarily concerned with football and the resurgence of the Green Bay Packers.

The Packers were changing as they headed into the 1970 season. Herb Adderly, a great cornerback for the Packers, during a career that spanned ten years, blamed the coaching staff because he wasn't picked for the post-season Pro Bowl game, and asked to be traded. Elijah Pitts, Lee Roy Caffey, and Bob Hyland were traded to the Bears. Petty annoyances upset some of the players, and the military discipline and training practices instituted by Vince Lombardi had broken down under Coach Bengtson.

Despite the obvious breakdown of discipline, the team went through the 1970 exhibition season in fine style, winning all of its exhibition games. But then along toward the end of the summer there was news of Lombardi's grave illness, his hospitalization and obvious serious condition, and then his sudden death. Many of the players—all the Packers who played under Lombardi—flew to New York and attended services for the beloved coach at St. Patrick's Cathedral.

All the Packers were there, new and old team members, and the Washington Redskins, his new team, and a great many other football stars who had respected and admired him.

"But after we got back to Green Bay," said Ray Nitschke, a Packer linebacker for fifteen years, "something seemed to go out of the team. We had to try to get ready for our opening game against Detroit. Now with Lombardi gone and a lot of the faces that had been so familiar when he was coaching were gone—it was another year for us. Now, without Lombardi, it was another era for football."

Lambeau Field, the Packers' home field, had just been expanded, and 56,263 fans jammed the new facility. It was the largest home crowd ever to watch the Packers as they prepared to battle the Detroit Lions in the opening game of the season.

For the first time in history, the Packers failed to score at home as the Lions trampled over the Packers 40–0. It was a nightmare for the Packers as the cheers at the opening kickoff turned to boos as the defense failed time after time to stop the Lions' attack.

The team improved greatly after that first game, whipping Atlanta, Minnesota, San Diego—three fine victories in a row—and managed to end a lackluster season with victories over Philadelphia and the Pittsburgh Steelers to finally wind up with 6 victories, 8 losses.

Coach Bengtson had his second losing season out of three. He was a disciple of Lombardi. He knew what happens to losing coaches. He'd been an important part of those great Packer years, molding a defense that was the strongest in the league. But winning really is the only thing that counted, and Bengtson was fired as head coach and a new era was at hand.

Dan Devine, at age forty-six, was a year older than Vince Lombardi had been when he came to Green Bay. But whereas Lombardi had come with a reputation to make out of a lifetime of doubt and insecurity, Devine brought a sixteen-year record—120 victories, 40 losses, 8 tie games as head coach at Arizona State for three years and Missouri for thirteen.

"We've got a new coach," said Packer backfield star Bob Jeter, "and we've got the veterans here who still know how to win. Fellows like Carroll Dale, Lional Aldridge, Ken Bowman, Gale Gillingham, Jim Grabowski, Ray Nitschke, Donny Anderson, Dave Robinson, Willie Wood, Zeke Bratkowski, and Bart Starr."

Jeter may have been right, but Bart, injured again and hurting, was in and out of the line-up. All those jarring tackles by opposing tacklers were catching up to Bart after fifteen of the most brilliant years in professional football and unhappily Bart could not play often enough in this, his final year as an active player.

"As Bart Starr goes, so go the Packers," is what all the sportswriters were typing for their columns in the sports pages.

Bart Starr went well enough in the few games he played in 1971, but not nearly enough to change the Green Bay Packers' record in the win and loss results. In the first year of that thoroughly capable coach, Dan Devine, with the Wisconsin club, Green Bay suffered its worst record since 1958. All they could eke out of that disastrous season was 4 wins, while they lost 8 and managed to tie 2.

Bart went into the hospital.

Twice he was operated on, for that separated shoulder.

The doctors advised him to turn in his uniform.

His wife said, "You'll play as long as you want to play."

Bart wanted to play. If he could, he would play forever.

He tested his arm. He tried to throw with the old snap and precision, but just could not. Something was missing. His arm and shoulder ached with pain, and he could not put the ball into the air beyond twenty yards with any speed or accuracy. He was finished.

"The Lord takes care of such things," he said, but no one knew better than he did that his active days on the football field, as the top quarterback for the Packers, was over. In July of 1972, Bart sent a letter to the front office of the Green Bay Packers. It stated, simply, unhappily, he must retire from the active roster of the Packers.

But Bart had said, and said so often, "I love the game." How was he to leave it?

True, he could no longer lead his teammates onto the playing field. He could no longer take the snap from center, step back, read the defense, then toss that sure and pinpoint pass for a short gain, a long gain, the bomb. But football was in his blood. It was too much a part of him. And he would be back. Bart Starr would be back in the game, and he would make his presence felt.

In 1972, the honors kept rolling in for the magnificent quarterback. Again, the President of the United States appointed him a member of the President's Council on Physical Fitness. The President, too, appointed him a member of the President's Advisory Committee on Environmental Protection. He was asked to—with his wife, Cherry—chair the State Cancer Crusade. He chaired and continues to chair the Vincent Lombardi Memorial Golf Classic.

He was awarded the Wisconsin Writers' Association Meritorious Service Award. The Wisconsin Broadcasters' Association awarded him the Wisconsinite of the Year Award.

There would be more awards for both his civil contributions and his football feats. He was honored by the Columbus Touchdown Club for his feats on the gridiron that year, and all the years before, as the Professional Player of the Decade. The President of the United States took time out of his busy duties and responsibilities to personally attend a Bart Starr Testimonial Dinner in Green Bay. It was a marvelous tribute to Bart Starr . . . a night he and Cherry would never forget.

CHAPTER 25

Bart Starr's retirement from football did not last very long. He had retired as a player in July 1972, but he was back in August for the 1972 training camp, and, again, in a Green Bay Packer uniform—not as a player this time, but as an assistant coach, to handle the Packer quarterbacks. And, judging by the results, he did a top-notch job.

"The quarterback is the key man in any offense," said Vincent Lombardi and every other man who ever coached a football team. "Without an efficient quarterback, you have no attack."

Bart couldn't play that all-important quarterback position in 1972, lead the offensive thrust of the Packers, but he could impart his years of experience to Scott Hunter, the Packers' outstanding young quarterback. Hunter had a year's experience as a quarterback in 1971, and in addition had the added benefit of having Coach Bart Starr on the side line calling the plays. That kept some of the pressure off Scott. To his credit, Hunter listened carefully to everything Bart told him about quarterbacking and took advantage of this chance to learn from a master of the game.

Starr could call a close to perfect game, and Hunter was learning to execute the way Bart had. Watching the patterns develop on the field during the 1972 season, it sometimes seemed to onlookers that it was Starr out there instead of Hunter. And the result of his efforts was a winning season.

The biggest difference between the disastrous 1971 personnel and the 1972 team was Chester Marcol, who developed into the outstanding field-goal specialist in pro football. With Marcol on the squad, with such tremendous, hard-running backs as John Brockington and MacArthur Lane, the Packers were once again winners.

They took 10 of their 14 games for the best record since 1966, and the Central Division of the National Football League's championship as well. It was their first championship since 1967.

The Washington Redskins were too much for them in the Western Conference championship game, but there could be no doubt that Bart Starr had been a source of great inspiration for the bright showing of the Packers in 1972.

But, in January of 1973, for perhaps a variety of reasons, Bart again doffed the Green Bay Packer uniform. It may have been that as an assistant coach his moves, his action, his ideas on how to run a club were limited. Bart reported to the press that he could no longer neglect his business interests, which at this time were many.

There was the Acheson-Starr Enterprizes, with its two

very successful Lincoln-Mercury dealerships in Birmingham, Alabama. He was a member of the board of directors of the Sentry Insurance Company. He was constantly in demand as a speaker at business meetings, educational meetings, inspirational meetings. He was requested by any number of civil organizations to head a variety of finance-raising projects. He was tapped for any number of TV commercials, hosted a regional TV talk program, and was hired by CBS as a commentator for its football telecasts.

Bart Starr had enough to keep him busy, but he couldn't get away from football forever. Nor would the fans let him forget the game. In 1973 the Washington Touchdown Club honored him with the "Timmie" Award. It seemed that the football world was not going to let Bart Starr move very far from the gridiron.

At the end of 1974, following two disastrous seasons in 1973 and 1974, Dan Devine resigned as the Packer coach. Dan's tenure at Green Bay was stormy and controversial and—except for a 10–4 playoff team during his second year—unsuccessful.

Bart Starr applied for the job and was promptly appointed head coach of the Packers. It was a job he might have hesitated to take, for the story of great quarterbacks who became head coaches for professional football clubs is dismal. Otto Graham, Norm Van Brocklin, Sammy Baugh, Bob Waterfield, among the greatest in their time, failed miserably. But for Bart it may have been the challenge the job presented. More likely it was a dream he had nursed for a long time, which had at last come true.

"All I ask is prayers and patience," said Bart at the press conference, where he accepted a three-year contract as head coach and general manager of the Green Bay Packers, the day before Christmas 1974.

"We will earn everything else," he added.

There was the faith, the humility, the determination, all characteristic of the man in that statement.

"It may take a while," he said, "but it is my unequivocal pledge to give this organization a fresh start."

Bart had rejected any number of offers from any number of clubs in the past two years. One of those offers, it was rumored, came from the Los Angeles Rams and amounted to a million dollar package.

"I have a great love affair with the Packers," he said. "For one reason or another I could not get excited about going somewhere else. I always felt there would be a time and a place for me at Green Bay."

Nothing he said surprised the sportswriters at that press conference. It was Bart Starr as he had always been: modest, gentle, courteous, self-effacing, and eminently sincere.

"I've been a little disappointed the last few years in traveling around the country to see that some of the respect for the Green Bay Packers has slipped," he said.

"I want to help restore that prestige," he added, "the prestige that has been part of this team for so many years."

"I firmly believe," said the new Packer coach, "to every man there comes in his lifetime that special moment when he is figuratively tapped on the shoulder and offered that chance to do a very special thing, unique to him and fitted to his talents. What a tragedy if that moment finds him unprepared or unqualified for that work.

"I'm not as qualified as I'd like to be," he added, in his typical humble manner, "but I'm willing."

"Prayers and patience." That is what Bart asked for, and that was what he needed.

The sports pages were filled with the struggles and failures of former football heroes who returned to coach big-league football clubs.

The Detroit Lions, led by the Hall of Fame linebacker Joe Schmidt, never won a divisional championship. Hall of Fame wide receiver Tom Fears failed with the New Orleans Saints. Hall of Fame defensive back Jack Christiansen could take the San Francisco Forty-niners nowhere. Norm Van Brocklin missed with the Atlanta Falcons. Otto Graham was a failure with the Washington Redskins. Bob Waterfield never got anywhere with the Los Angeles Rams. Sammy Baugh took the New York Titans, as the New York Jets were called at the time, down the road to defeat.

Would Bart Starr follow in their path, or would he be able to break the pattern?

Bart began his attack on this pattern almost immediately. He said his most immediate task would be to eliminate the dissension rampant during Dan Devine's stormy four-year reign. "Everybody in this organization has to be pulling together," he said. "This league is too tough to allow for bickering and internal strife."

The only coach he retained of the Dan Devine regime was his old teammate Dave Hammer, who was in his twenty-fourth consecutive year with the Packers as player and coach. As a player, Dave won recognition as a five-time All-Pro selection during the early years of the Lombardi era. In 1965 Dave was appointed to the coaching staff by Vince Lombardi and quickly became known throughout the league as an outstanding defensive coach.

Bart hired another Packer teammate, Zeke Bratkowski, who had previously served as an assistant to Coach Bengtson in 1969 and 1970, before returning to active Packer duty as Bart Starr's backup quarterback in 1971. A veteran of some fourteen years in the NFL, Zeke had starred with the Chicago Bears and the Los Angeles Rams before coming to the Packers in 1963.

Lew Carpenter had been one of Green Bay's most versatile ballplayers from 1956 to 1963. He had starred for the Packers as a wide receiver, tight end, halfback, and fullback, and after his active playing days were over, Lew had served on the coaching staffs of the Vikings, Redskins, Atlanta Falcons, Cardinals, and the Houston Oilers before coming to the Packers.

And before the 1975 training sessions got under way, Bart began to cut from his squad those Green Bay gridders who were long past their prime—who, in fact, had never achieved a prime.

At camp, Bart installed a tough, precise routine.

"We have no illusions," he said for the press. "We have weaknesses to shore up and are thin in the ranks. We have a lot of work to do."

His players, strangely enough, adhered to Bart's strict rules and routines, and admired their coach for his firm and determined attitudes. Unfortunately, even the most grueling of training programs is not enough to mold a championship football team, and Bart Starr's squad was far from championship caliber.

Bart inherited a number of problems he would as soon have done without, but if they hadn't existed there might not have been a Green Bay coaching job open in the first place. The controversial trade in the middle of 1974 for quarterback John Hadl provided the Packers with an experienced quarterback but deprived them of first, second, and third choices in the 1975 college draft, and of first and second choices in 1976.

Another problem that Bart had to face was the 1975 deal for All-Pro linebacker Ted Hendricks. At Green Bay, Hendricks' salary jumped from $48,500 to $125,000 and his option clause was taken out of the Green Bay contract. As a result, when Hendricks wanted an additional increase, Bart traded him to Oakland.

Added to these problems, Gale Gillingham and the great cornerback Ken Ellis left the club. Perhaps the biggest blow was the injury to kicker Chester Marcol. Chet suffered a deep muscle pull—an injury that was to keep him on the sidelines all year long.

Bart had some depth at quarterback with John Hadl, but Jack Concannon and Jerry Tagge were of little help. In every other position the club was thin, and the defense had ranked no higher than fifth in the League in 1974.

"If you're going to win in the future," said Coach Bart Starr, "you have to build with a solid, rock-hard foundation."

The trouble was, and is, that fans want their teams to win now. They've very little mind for the future.

"I am very much interested in winning," said Bart, "but sometimes you can win with gimmickry. I don't want to do things that way. I want that solid foundation."

The trouble, again, is that fans really don't care too much to listen to plans for solid foundations. They want their teams to win any way they can, gimmickry or not.

The Green Bay Packers, under Coach Bart Starr, lost their first 4 games in 1975. It was a disastrous beginning for Bart, yet his faithful following, however disheartened, would not desert him.

Jerry Kramer, his old Packer buddy, says, "I have been watching Bart Starr for almost twenty years now, and I have been waiting to see him fall on his face, and he hasn't fallen yet. I don't expect him to start now."

In the season's fifth game the Packers came back to beat the Eastern Conference Division leaders, the Dallas Cowboys; and it was the first defeat the Cowboys had to suffer in the young season.

It was tradition and Bart Starr's own personal magic that worked as the Packers handed Dallas their first defeat in 5 games, 19–17.

The Packers were trailing 17–12 when Dallas' Golden Richards fumbled the ball and Steve Luke recovered for Green Bay on the Dallas 31-yard line with 2 minutes to go. On the second play, quarterback John Hadl lofted a 26-yard pass that Richie McGeorge caught and carried into the end zone for the winning points.

"I'm about three feet off the ground," said an elated Bart Starr after the game.

Green Bay would win, however, only 4 games through that 1975 schedule, and lose 10. It was not an auspicious beginning for Bart Starr as coach of the Green Bay Packers. But neither had his beginning for the Packers, as quarterback, been auspicious.

There was a great ray of hope and new enthusiasm in 1976 with the acquisition of the lanky, strong-armed quarterback, Lynn Dickey. Lynn had played with Houston for several years, but lacked the actual game experience necessary to be a top quarterback. Starr felt that he could work with Dickey, guide him, and play him enough to develop him into a top-notch quarterback. But early in the season Lynn was injured, and the Packers glittering hopes fell to zero.

The Packers managed however, to win 5 games, while losing 9. It was a slight improvement over 1975.

"In many ways," said Bart, "the past two seasons were a great deal like I had expected them to be. There was a lot of hard work, long hours, a restructuring of thoughts and ideas. There were a lot of areas in which I had to become familiar in a hurry."

Bart Starr was summing up the two dismal seasons. As always with Bart, if anything went wrong with a game or even an entire schedule, he would find the fault in himself first.

"Cherry," he said, speaking of his wife, "tells me that I'm not quite as patient as I used to be."

He smiled. "Maybe she is right."

"There is a lot to be learned in an adverse situation,"

he continued, referring of course to a losing season. "I think you learn a lot about people and about yourself in a losing situation, and that's good. That should help us all in the future."

This was the religious Bart Starr speaking, his sense that all men are essentially good.

"I feel that the single most important ingredient to achieving," he continued, "is developing and maintaining the proper attitude. Our people were able to overcome a number of handicaps and setbacks because they were able to display this kind of attitude."

He was finding the kind of words for his players. Saying the kind word about others may be difficult for some; for Bart Starr it comes naturally. He was thinking particularly of the Packers' defeat of the Dallas Cowboys, the team that had gone on to win the National Football League 1975 championship.

But if Bart enjoyed talking about the few happy moments in his first two years as coach of the Packers, he did not avoid the unpleasant memories, the numerous defeats.

"I think all of us are embarrassed by the record, and incensed. I hope we are. It's going to make us work harder to come out of this the best way we can next year. This record is hanging over our heads. It's something we all have to live with because our names are on it. It's something we have to make up for."

A fan, writing to the Packers, summarized the feelings of Green Bay about their club—and especially Bart Starr.

"The Packers," he wrote, "have had two tough years.

Injuries, retirement, and rotten luck have really spelled havoc on the win-loss column. However, the thing that impressed me most is that the team never let itself get down. I think this is to the credit of Bart Starr.

"The Pack is on the right step back and all the fans need now is a little patience, and to give Coach Starr a chance."

Bart Starr had asked for prayers and patience, when he took on the job of Green Bay's coach. There are many, in addition to Bart, who pray. Patience, on the other hand, is a sometimes virtue.

Bart had an acronym for success:

S—Sense of direction,
U—Understanding,
C—Charity,
C—Courage,
E—Esteem,
S—Self-confidence,
S—Sense of humor.

It is an acronym he has offered at countless dinners and banquets as well as at the many meetings in which he has delivered inspirational messages to the young people. He invented the acronym and it is an acronym whose definition he wholly believes and trusts. It is also an acronym that spells out best, perhaps, the character of that great quarterback.

He doesn't have to prove any more how great a gridder he was in his playing days. He still has to prove himself a great coach but, with patience and prayer, there can be no doubt about his ultimate success. According to anybody who knows football, its players and its history, if anyone can succeed as a coach on the gridiron, it must be, it has to be Mr. Quarterback himself, Bryan Bartlett Starr.

GENE SCHOOR has been associated with sports and sports personalities since his high school days in Passaic, New Jersey. After winning a number of amateur boxing championships in New Jersey, Gene received an athletic scholarship to Miami University (Florida) where the boxing team became contenders for the national championships during the years that Schoor was a member of the team. Gene captured some eighteen regional boxing championships and fought his way to the final round of the 1940 Olympics as a welterweight, only to lose his post on the team due to a broken hand.

Mr. Schoor has been a teacher and boxing coach at both the University of Minnesota and City College, New York, and was also a sports commentator on radio stations WINS, WNBC, and WHN. He has produced and directed radio and television programs with Joe DiMaggio and Jack Dempsey. Currently, he is devoting his efforts to his writing career and has published a number of books with the best selling author, Robin Moore. The author of forty books, Schoor has written biographies of many of the nation's greatest sports and political figures including: *Vince Lombardi—Football's Greatest Coach, Bob Feller—Strikeout King, The Story of Yogi Berra, The Jackie Robinson Story, The Jim Thorpe Story, The Story of Willie Mays, Leo Durocher, Young John Kennedy, Young Robert Kennedy, The Story of Franklin D. Roosevelt, General Douglas MacArthur, Sugar Ray Robinson, Roy Campanella, Treasury of Notre Dame Football, Treasury of Army-Navy Football,* and other books of note.